IGOR

The Courage of Chernobyl's Child

UPDATED

*for the 20th Anniversary
of the Chernobyl Disaster*

By Jane Warren

IGOR: The Courage of Chernobyl's Child – UPDATED

Published by Emanuel Imprints

ISBN: 0-9552264-0-6 / 978-0-9552264-0-3

First edition published in Great Britain by Boxtree Ltd., London in 1996

Typeset by Able Publishing, Knebworth, Hertfordshire
www.ablepublishing.co.uk

Printed in Great Britain by Impress Print, Northampton

Cover Design: www.zilvester.com

For Elena and Andre Pavlovets

Jane Warren is an author and a senior feature writer at the *Daily Express*. She lives in West Sussex with her husband, Willem, and one-year-old daughter, Bea.

Her other books include:

- *The Ali Abbas Story: The Moving Story of One Boy's Struggle for Life* (HarperCollins, 2004)
- *Fear Busting: A Proven Plan to Beat Fear and Change Your Life*, with Pete Cohen (Element, 2003)
- *Simply Ayurveda: Discover Your Type to Transform Your Life*, with Bharti Vyas (Thorsons, 2000)
- *One Up: A Woman in Action with the SAS*, with Sarah Ford (HarperCollins, 1997)
- *A Self-Made Man: The Diary of a Man Born in a Woman's Body*, with Paul Hewitt (Headline, 1995)

Contents

Author's Note and Acknowledgements

2006 is the 20th anniversary of the world's worst nuclear accident. It also marks 10 years since Igor: The Courage of Chernobyl's Child was first published.

Much has happened in that time. Igor is now nineteen years old. In 2003, at the age of sixteen, he was reunited with his birth parents, about whom nothing was known for many years. At the time of original publication it was assumed that, unable to cope with his disability, they had chosen to abandon him at birth and this was the speculative perspective from which the first edition of this book was written.

Now the full story of how they were forced to give him up as part of the then Soviet Union's cover-up of the Chernobyl disaster can at last be told, and I am grateful to Elena Pavlovets for her trust in allowing me to tell it on her behalf. In this new edition, the original book, revised and with speculative passages excised, is followed by an extensive update based on interviews with Elena and with Victor Mizzi, the chairman of Chernobyl Children Life Line, who reunited mother and son.

I remain grateful to Richard Compton Miller for his introduction to Boxtree, who commissioned the original book. Thank you Victor for inviting me to update it for the 20th anniversary and for bringing Elena from Belarus to visit me. A special thank you to my treasured husband, Willem Mulder, for the cover artwork, and for his support in looking after Bea whilst I was working on the update. I remain grateful to all the interviewees and contacts who assisted with the original book and who were acknowledged there.

Igor, I hope this book will satisfy your desire for a final and definitive account of the past. Thank you for allowing me to write about you, once again.

Jane Warren, December 2005

Foreword to the First Edition

by the Rt Hon Virginia Bottomley MP

I am only too conscious of the anxiety suffered by parents who look after handicapped children, and of their grief when their children are ill. Jane Warren's important book tells the moving story of Igor Pavlovets who was born with profound deformities as a consequence of the Chernobyl disaster 10 years ago.

I have met children from the region near Chernobyl on many occasions and have always been impressed by their behaviour and courage. Among them, Igor stands out. His spirited cheerfulness is an inspiration to us all. Igor was born with few advantages, but has overcome his predicament in a way that could move the coldest heart. He is able to lead a normal life and take part in all the activities children enjoy, and always with such enthusiasm.

The people who undertake the responsibility of helping such children are worthy of the highest praise. Many people have good intentions, but a family who open their home, as Roy and Barbara Bennett have done for Igor, are examples to us all. I am proud that a British charity was able to see his potential. Without the intervention of Chernobyl Children Lifeline, Igor would still be living in an institution with no prospect of a future. The Charity does tremendous work in helping the unfortunate children of the Republic of Belarus, which received 70 per cent of the contamination after the disaster. It has helped to create a better understanding between our society and theirs, and given a ray of hope to this stricken region.

I know Igor will do well in life. His courage and his personality will see him through the difficult years yet to come. Yet he will always remind us of the terrible accident and of the importance of trying to leave our children a better, safer world.

The House of Commons, March 1996

The Cartwheel

It was Igor's first day at school. Out of the corner of his eye, the seven-year-old could see Mrs Reid preparing to raise her hand to signal the end of break and the end of his game. The teacher's arm shot into the air like a flagpole. The other children ran over to line up patiently next to her, but Igor stayed on the far side of the playground, took a deep breath and set off on a sequence of magnificent one-handed cartwheels across the width of the tarmac. The other children watched in excitement as he propelled his agile little body with his powerful arm. They broke into laughter and clapped their hands as the schoolboy acrobat bounced onto his feet and waved, before falling into line with them. Igor bellowed with laughter and basked in the attention. The children fell in love with him, he was so cheerful and happy.

Igor's left arm, his muscular cartwheel arm, is perfectly formed. But he has no right arm. If you saw him swimming you'd notice a small knot of muscle near his right shoulder, and nothing more. His legs are very short, and inside his custom-built shoes are more puzzles. His left foot has just two, extra-long toes. His right foot has three.

Igor is a happy boy with a glorious smile. He is also extremely intelligent. His unusual congenital disabilities were caused by the world's worst nuclear disaster, 1600 kilometres away from this typical English school playground, when Chernobyl reactor number four melted down in the former USSR on 26 April 1986. The story of how Igor became an English schoolboy is compelling and heartbreaking in equal measure.

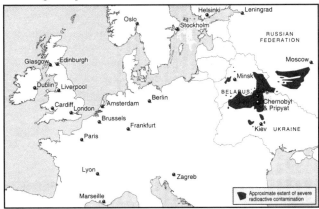

The Disaster

There was already a fire in the core of the reactor and flames were licking the roof like angry tongues, when the phone shrilled at the home of Leonid, the nuclear reactor's fire chief. It was the control room, ringing in desperation. Leonid glanced at his clock: 1.25 a.m. He scrambled out of bed. There was an orange glow across the rye and flax fields. The Chernobyl power station, a towering structure of concrete and steel, had seemed invulnerable but now the fire had taken hold and was lighting up the night sky.

Leonid grabbed his red helmet and leather gloves. He quickly dressed and, still doing up the brass buttons on his heavy coat, raced to the reactor, which was spitting fragments of metal and concrete from the roof. It was a warm spring night, made hotter by the boiling debris he was forced to dodge as he darted inside the power plant through the heavy door. He ran past the faded safety posters stuck on the walls of the concrete passage, his attention focused on the smoke pouring from beneath the door of the reactor room. He turned the metal handle, pulled open the door and was almost knocked off his feet by a blast of boiling air. He shielded his eyes with his leather gloved hands and peered into the inferno, then ran back to the passage and phoned for assistance from other fire stations in the area. His team of twenty-eight men and three fire engines wasn't equipped to tackle this alone.

Leonid, who was in his thirties, knew that just by standing in the burning reactor he was gravely endangering his health, but he also knew that it was imperative to try to stop the fire spreading to one or more of the other three reactors. Each of them was the size of an aircraft carrier and the consequences of further explosions were too terrible to consider.

Leonid ran back outside. By now the area was crawling with poorly equipped fire trucks, all sounding their noisy klaxons. Their water jets were puny splashes against the white-hot inferno. They looked like crawling beetles next to the sky-scraping walls. Leonid scrambled seventy metres up a metal ladder to the roof of the burning reactor to direct operations. By now, the members of his fire-crew were shouting to each other over the roar of the flames as they peered into the gaping mouth in the fractured roof. Completely dwarfed by the scale of the reactor, they were just tiny figures scurrying across the top of the flaming building, using picks and shovels to scrape fragments into the crater. Everything was confusion.

Smoke obscured the striped red and white chimney towering above the reactor and the soot made it difficult to breathe. Feeling his boots sticking to the roof, Leonid looked down at his feet. The black bitumen sealing the roof against the rain had melted because of the high temperatures and was starting to blister. He tore his feet from the gummy tar surface just in time. Moments after he began his hazardous descent from the roof, it collapsed completely. Flames leapt like rockets into the sky above the plant. Hundreds of smaller fires were ignited as burning debris and bitumen were thrown up and then smashed to the ground. Limbs of twisted metal were burning. Broken concrete lay in smoking boulders. Before the catastrophe, the most the serious blaze Leonid had tackled was a peat fire in a local shop. But despite his inexperience, the brave fire chief and his men stayed on the front line to battle with the blaze. They worked on autopilot. This was their duty to their country, and to their families still sleeping so close by. Even after they had put out the flames, however, the reactor would continue to smoulder for weeks.

Meanwhile, deep in the heart of the burning reactor, an engineer called Alexei was working feverishly in the control room. He had been there when the reactor exploded, after senior officers had ordered a precarious experiment to see if it could run on low power. They had shut off the safety systems and ignored the red alert and flashing lights. And now this: the core had become unstable and soared in temperature to 3000 degrees centigrade, as hot as the molten heart of a volcano. The fuel pipes had buckled, causing an explosion of such force it had blasted the lid off the reactor, killing several workers nearby.

Alexei began to press buttons to shut down the other three reactors. Like Leonid, he knew it was vital to do what he could to prevent another explosion, so he remained for four more hours. He concentrated hard, sweating with the effort of trying to bring the stricken reactor under control; it was like defusing a time bomb. Soon he felt strangely unwell. Within the first two hours after the explosion, he had to rush out of the control room to be sick in the corridor, which was swirling with smoke. The fifty-five year-old understood the dangers and he knew that his nausea was the first symptom of massive radiation poisoning. The fire in the reactor's heart was pumping out a lethal cocktail of radioactive isotopes and to remain in the vicinity was to accept a death sentence, but he forced himself to ignore the signs. He had to leave the cooling systems for the other three reactors operational, otherwise they too could melt down and explode.

Once Alexei had made them as safe as he could, he ran out of the control room. Behind him, large portions of the walls of reactor number four were caving in. As he slammed the heavy metal door and ran out under the dawn sky, Alexei had received three times the fatal dose of radiation. Feeling dizzy and weak, he looked up. A thick black cloud of smoke was stretching out from the reactor across the sky like a motorway, carrying 190 tonnes of lethal radioactive material across the countryside.

Several hours after the meltdown, the area was swarming with thirty-seven fire brigades and a total of 186 firemen. The Soviet Minister for Energy had been told only of 'a small defect' at the reactor, which had been built to provide power for heavy industry such as refineries and metal foundries, but for nine days the invisible killer would silently pour from the crumbled reactor. Translated from Russian, Chernobyl means 'black truth', and the black truth of the Chernobyl disaster was radiation.

If a nuclear reactor vessel is destroyed, huge quantities of highly radioactive nuclear fuel can escape and pollute the environment. Water, soil, plants and animals will all absorb the radioactive material and living creatures will suffer as a result. The most frightening thing about radiation is that we have no senses to detect it. Neither sight nor hearing, touch, taste nor smell will warn you of even fatal levels. You can't boil contaminated water or cook contaminated food to make it safe, and once radioactive isotopes are inside the body they will remain lodged in vital organs for decades, emitting radiation as they decay. This will corrupt the vital genetic code of cells. If the contamination is great enough, it is only a matter of time before a corrupted cell becomes cancerous, especially inside a child's body. And a field containing radioactive material will produce contaminated food for hundreds of years.

Nuclear power is supposed to be cheap to produce because the raw fuel is less expensive than oil, gas or coal. But the rigorous safety requirements for operating a reactor and handling the spent fuel make it one of the most expensive sources of energy in the developed world. So the Soviets cut corners. Most of their reactors have no safety shields. Neither do they have sufficient automatic shutdown systems that would operate in the event of disaster. The Soviets thought these were superfluous frills, and even mocked other countries for being over-cautious with their safety procedures. They boasted that their nuclear reactors were of a superior design despite the fact British experts had condemned reactors like the one at Chernobyl as unsafe thirty years before the disaster.

The local people didn't know any of this. All information about power plants in the Soviet Union was controlled by the secret police, who kept the real truth about Soviet nuclear power to themselves. So on the fateful night of the meltdown, the control-room staff who weren't directly involved with the experiment were probably not watching their instruments. They had been led to believe that nothing could go wrong. They were told repeatedly during their training that 'a nuclear power plant cannot explode'.

The first sign of impending disaster was probably a warning light. Winking on the control panel, it would have signalled that something was wrong with the water-cooling system. The nuclear reactors at Chernobyl needed to have cold water pumped through their pipes to prevent them overheating. But while the operators ignored the flashing light, water was actually seeping into the reactor's core. This rapidly turned into steam and a deadly chain reaction began. The temperature of the core soared and the huge vessel containing the core of the reactor erupted. An up-rush of volatile hydrogen gas was released and ignited as it mixed with the air above the core. The roof was blown off the building and burning debris started fires. The experiment had run out of control and destroyed the reactor vessel, threatening millions of lives. But rather than admitting what had happened, the General Secretary of the Soviet Union, Mikhail Gorbachev, covered up details of the disaster. He didn't want the news to reach the outside world. But he couldn't hide the radiation. The day after the explosion, 1300 kilometres north of the Chernobyl reactor, the Swedish government discovered exceptionally high levels of radiation during a routine air-quality check. Gorbachev was then forced to admit the problem to other governments, but he was vague, referring simply to 'a small accident'. He neglected to tell his own people anything; on the television and radio news there was barely a mention. Most people didn't realise how serious the situation was because everything was kept secret.

It took only hours for Alexei's radiation sickness to start. Soon his skin was itching and breaking into blisters that made him look as if he had run through fire. A disturbing sweet taste filled his mouth. Within days, his hair, like Leonid's, was falling out in clumps. Then he collapsed. Alexei was later driven to Moscow's City Hospital Six, where he was shrouded in a plastic sheet called a 'life island' that covered him from head to toe. His body was undergoing a total shutdown.

Radiation destroys the marrow at the heart of the bones so it can no longer produce new blood cells. There is also internal bleeding. The body's ability to fight off infection is wiped out, so even a cold or a minor scratch can prove fatal to someone who has absorbed too much radiation. From beneath the plastic, Alexei looked up at his family when they came to visit him in hospital. They weren't allowed to touch him because his skin was so sore it would have made him cry out. Alexei's hair had fallen out by now and his skin was a blotchy mahogany colour. Black blisters on his hands and face had turned red, and were weeping. Alexei had the same stoic but frightened look as terminally ill cancer patients. When he died, he was a hero. A few weeks later Leonid, the brave fire chief, also died of radiation poisoning. Were it not for their efforts, the reactor core might have melted down even further and caused greater devastation.

The government still hadn't admitted that there had been a disaster at Chernobyl. They hadn't revealed the truth about the fire still smouldering in the reactor, or that there was a molten lake of radioactive soup at its core emitting deadly vapour, or even that the land was slowly being poisoned by fall-out, the radioactive debris which drops from the sky and scatters over the ground after a nuclear explosion. So school children living nearby played outside during morning break without a clue of the dangers. Meanwhile, convoys of trucks had started streaming up and down the road to Chernobyl. When they got within thirty kilometres of the plant, they dumped their weighty deliveries of sand, cement and lead. The cargoes were then transferred to trucks already contaminated with radiation. These rumbled up the road to the plant where the materials were once again off-loaded, this time to plug the volcano.

Twenty-five Soviet helicopter pilots flew suicide missions, 250 metres above the burning reactor. The aircraft looked like mechanical flies, dwarfed by the reactor as the pilots tried to dodge the plumes of dense radioactive smoke spewing into the sky. They flew in as low as they could to dive-bomb the burning reactor with sand to extinguish the fires, or boron, a brown chemical, to suppress the continuous nuclear reactions. The pilots had no anti-radiation suits to wear and had never before tried to put out a nuclear fire. All they could do was grabs sheets of lead from the lorries and place them on the seats of their helicopters to act as feeble protection against the radiation shining out from the reactor. The pilots dumped so much sand as the weeks went by that American satellite pictures showed it spilling out all around the reactor. A new mission then had to begin to stop the reactor sinking through its foundations.

Initially, the pilots were working alongside ten robots lent by Germany and Japan. These robots shifted lumps of radioactive debris from the reactor's core and the roof, but they were soon useless. Radiation levels were so high that their circuitry began to malfunction. They either raced out of control and slammed into walls, or hurled themselves off the disintegrating roof. To replace them, President Gorbachev made a grim and calculated decision. He ordered the job to be finished by human hand. Teams of young men from all over the Soviet Union were ordered to do the work of the robots. Dressed in lead suits and glass visors, these 'bio-robots' began the laborious clean up with shovels. They were just farmers, miners and factory workers, simple men who knew little of radiation but had the muscle power to work at speed. Their supervisors made a cursory attempt to limit the men's exposure to levels of radiation that were so high that they could kill immediately. The men were given sixty seconds to rush up the ramp to the top of the reactor, grab a shovel and push two chunks of radioactive debris into the core. This was supposed to limit their exposure to the most radioactively hot areas to five seconds.

They would also swarm around the base of the power plant, shovelling debris into piles and scooping it up into trucks, which would then drive to one of the six hundred dumpsites within the contaminated zone to bury their radioactive load. Eventually the trucks themselves would be buried in these shallow graves. Piles of earth and stones were excavated at the sites, but because the job was done so quickly they were neither deep enough nor well enough covered to be safe. These brave men, known as 'the liquidators', worked day and night to bury the crippled reactor itself. A vast Soviet army of over half a million men was conscripted to work at the disaster site over the coming year. The men were told that the faster they ran, the safer they would be, so they responded by shedding their lead trousers and aprons, which had made it impossible to move, and got on with the deadly job as hastily as they could. They were then dressed only in thin white cotton overalls that provided no protection, and cumbersome helmets that would mist up on the inside of the glass. They kept the helmets on because they were told that to breathe the vapour would kill them instantly.

As they began to construct a concrete sarcophagus over the top of the damaged reactor, all the workers had soon received a lifetime's dose of radiation. To create the shroud, they used 6,000 tonnes of steel for the metal superstructure and coated it with a concrete wall a metre thick. The plan was that it would seal off the reactor and stop the radiation seeping into the atmosphere. The men also scraped off the top twenty centimetres of soil from the area around the plant and replaced it with concrete slabs. They chopped down forests of contaminated silver birch trees. They bulldozed farms and villages. Everything was badly buried by men who didn't understand the need for absolute precision. Yet Mikhail Gorbachev's government officials still insisted that radiation levels were low and everything was under control.

At night the brave liquidators slept in rest huts protected by layers of lead sheeting. They were given certificates from the government which proclaimed them to be heroes in the 'fight' against the 'enemy' of radiation. But soon the liquidators began to collapse. Hundreds have since died and thousands are seriously ill with terminal cancers. Despite the fact that the power station was lethally radioactive, the government ferried in nuclear scientists from all over the Soviet Union to operate the other three reactors at Chernobyl, all of which were soon restarted.

The Evacuation

Just six hours after the explosion, people were waking up to an overcast Saturday morning in the Belarussian villages and towns north-west of Chernobyl. They knew nothing of the overnight disaster and were simply looking forward to an afternoon spent in the forests, gathering mushrooms and picking berries, but as they stepped outside something felt quite wrong. In the sky a dark cloud cast a shadow over the cabbage and potato fields. A hostile wind scurried into eddies and whipped up the grass. And on the paths outside their houses, on the roads, in the playgrounds, a strange black dirt had settled. The air tasted of the ugly gritty powder. The children didn't know what it was, so they decided it must be black snow. But this snow was different. It stained their hands and clothes.

The children who lived in the bustling town of Pripyat, in northern Ukraine, were in a state of agitation the morning after the reactor exploded for their parents had forbidden them to go outside to play. They were among the 55,000 residents of the town that had sprung up a couple of kilometres from the Chernobyl reactor. Nearly a decade earlier, the engineers building the power station had arrived at the small pastoral community of wooden houses, bringing their wives and children. Shops had opened, schools were built and a hospital constructed. Gradually a prosperous town of high-rise apartment blocks had developed, and was said to be the most modern town in the Soviet Union, but it was a community completely dependent on the two-faced charms of a nuclear power station.

The children watched the shimmering flames, fire trucks and dive-bombing helicopters from the windows of their two-room apartments nearby. Many of their fathers worked at the reactor and were courageously attempting to combat the toxic fires. Some of the children had been told not to open the windows, so they had to look at the fireworks through the steamed-up glass. Soon they were growing restless. They were told to keep their shoes on inside the apartments. Some of them were given small white tablets. Many parents in Pripyat decided to keep their children home from school on Monday; those that went were sent home by their teachers. Then the government ordered the people of Pripyat to evacuate their town immediately. Everyone was bewildered and disorientated. Told to walk five kilometres out of town, they were forbidden to carry anything with them. They left their toys, schoolbooks, clothes and furniture. They tried to be brave, despite the frightening circumstances. As they reached the forests outside the town they saw hundreds of buses waiting for them, exhaust fumes drifting among the trees. Within thirty-six hours of the disaster the entire population had been bussed away and Pripyat became a ghost town. People were forced to depart with such urgency that beds were unmade, breakfast was still on the table and washing up was piled in the sink. The evacuated residents were driven to a tented city near Slavutich, 100 kilometres away. They were ordered to remove their clothing, which was burned, and they were then led into flapping canvas tents for decontamination before entering army showers. Even their roubles were exchanged for new money; the old notes and coins were buried.

In 2006, David Hughes, a writer for the Sunday Telegraph magazine, returned to Pripyat to report on this 20th-century Pompeii. He found a town frozen in time and gradually turning green. 'Small forests already reach to the top of apartment blocks. Inside buildings, trees grow through floors. The football pitch in the town stadium is now thick with 30ft-high pines. The surrounding farmland is now overgrown meadow, full of waist-high reeds and grasses,' he wrote.

In the Belarussian city of Gomel, 160 kilometres north east of the reactor, the local Communist party issued an order that everyone should stay within the confines of their apartment blocks. Then, four days after the disaster, when the pressure of waiting inside had grown to boiling point, the government suddenly claimed the situation was 'stable'. They said the residents of Gomel and other towns nearby were free to go outside to join in the traditional May Day celebrations. There was collective relief at the news.

It had been raining lightly, and now the warm sun was filtering through the clouds. The families streamed into the parks and prepared to celebrate with the costumes, banners and flags they had made during the previous weeks. A lot of black dust lay on the ground, turned to mud by the spring rain. It stuck to their shoes, so they wiped it off unaware that it was contaminated material from the sky. When the parades in the towns and cities cheerfully set off, most people were wearing light summery clothes, grateful to feel the warmth on their skin after days spent cooped up inside. But when the crowds cheerfully marched past the parade stand where the city leaders and army officials usually sat, they witnessed a sinister fancy dress party. Every person there was dressed in crisp white cotton suits. Fabric helmets like beekeeper's hats were draped over their heads down to their shoulders. Over their faces were smoky glass visors. With a chill, the marching locals realised that these were radiation suits. They looked at their children's bare arms and were felt terrified.

After the explosion, the authorities had pulled out charts and drawn a circle extending thirty kilometres around the reactor. Anyone living inside this 'dead zone' would have to leave. But it is impossible to draw a neat line around a radiation zone, however important the person looking at the map. The deadly cloud was drifting further north across 1600 kilometres of north-western Europe. The nuclear fall-out it was carrying was blown by the wind, settling on the ground and seeping into the nearby water meadows, sand flats and silver birch and pine forests. It was gradually being absorbed into the water supply and entering the food chain.

The officials sent radiation experts swarming over the countryside to measure the levels with specialised machinery. Sometimes the experts found 'hot spots' – areas of lethally high contamination sixty to eighty kilometres from the reactor. Where the levels of radiation were found to be off the scale the maps were marked with a purple patches and soon looked like bodies covered in painful bruises. Yet at other times, the men with the Geiger counters found patches of land within sight of the reactor that didn't register on the dial. Radiation was unpredictable. It did not respect boundaries.

Gradually the order came through that the outlying communities would have to be evacuated as well. In the villages near Pripyat, the villagers knew something terrible had happened. They had seen busloads of refugees travelling at speed along the main roads. They had seen the ominous black clouds hanging in the sky. But they didn't understand what had happened at the power station that had brought the miracle of electricity into their wooden houses 12 years earlier.

These were country people. They had lived all their lives on the fertile plains of southern Belarus, growing crops of potatoes, cabbages and beans. At first, they refused the orders to leave. There were hills between them and the reactor, natural shields that would protect them from anything nasty in the next valley. It was impossible for many of them to grasp the scale and extent of radiation's malignant reach and so Soviet civil servants were sent into the villages to explain that to stay could be fatal. The villagers' children had grown up on milk from their cows, eggs from their chickens and meat from their pigs. Now they were being told that they should no longer eat these things. They found it impossible to believe that their homegrown produce, which looked as nutritious and healthy as ever, could be poison. It was impossible to believe that they were being told to abandon villages where their families had lived for generations and they explained to the experts that they wouldn't leave without their cattle.

Only when the local government officials promised to bring in high-sided trucks to evacuate their cows with them, did the villagers even consider leaving.

They reluctantly agreed when they were told that the village leaders could ride in the trucks with the animals to make sure no harm came to them.

The evacuations of the 5,000 people in the forbidden zone were lethally slow and some villagers were not moved until four years after the accident. There was little that could be done to make the people safe. The small white tablets that some of the children in Pripyat had been given contained stable iodine, an element that is taken up by the thyroid gland, preventing it from absorbing radioactive iodine. Most adults were given nothing to counteract the effects.

While the villages were being steadily stripped of human life, the contaminated cloud continued to blow across the countryside. So in cities near the reactor another convoy had begun in the weeks after the disaster. In the city of Kiev half a million children were bussed out of the city, sent on enforced holidays far from the radioactive parks and the contaminated water supply. All adults were left behind. As their buses drove them away from the city, the children looked out of the windows at the peculiar sight of rolls of colourful carpet lining the streets of their beautiful city, placed there to damp down radiation. Splashes of water sprayed the bus windows from the sprinklers set up to wash the city – the officials had ordered this to be done three times daily. Dousing every pavement and every building up to the level of the first floor was the only way they knew to try to deal with the radioactive dust. As the buses drove past check-points encircling the city, the children could see men in rubber breathing gear and protective clothing monitoring the cars driving into the town for radioactivity. Any vehicle found to exceed the limit was being turned away.

It felt so strange in Kiev once the thousands of children had left. People had no choice but to try to keep living as normally as possible. They walked in the parks and fished in the River Dnieper, despite being warned not to. The schools were abandoned and the playgrounds silent, lemonade-dispensing machines in the centre of town were deserted and the many ice-cream stalls were shuttered up. In the parks, babushkas – well-built elderly women wearing traditional white headscarves – were cutting grass to make hay as they did every year. Although they had been told it contained deadly isotopes and would be buried, the babushkas continued to scythe. It seemed important to keep up with tradition and maintain some normality in the face of such confusion. In the market places, anxious peasant women displayed their potatoes and onions, but on top of the scrubbed wooden tables were new additions to their stalls – small white certificates neatly initialled by the market director. These showed that the produce on sale had just passed the scrutiny of a radiation test after feverish washing.

In hospitals across the Soviet Union many of the liquidators who had fought so courageously against the burning reactor were now dying. There was nothing the doctors could do to stop their bodies decaying. They weren't equipped to handle such a disaster. Then American multi-millionaire, Dr Armand Hammer, who enjoyed close links with the Soviet Union, had a sudden inspiration. Sitting inside his house overlooking the crashing waves of a Californian beach and reading about the nuclear disaster on the other side of the world, he wondered whether bone-marrow transplants could aid the dying men. The cells that radiation kills first are those that grow fastest – the ones inside the mouth, the stomach, and the bones. Because cancerous cells divide the quickest of all this is why controlled dosages of radiation are often used to treat cancer. A bone-marrow transplant is an operation where the soft centre of the hipbone from a healthy patient is gently sucked out and injected into the bone of an ill patient. The theory is that the healthy person's bone marrow will increase rapidly, replacing the diseased and radioactive material. It is a little like throwing seeds on newly turned earth: hopefully, some of the healthy cells will take root and the body will again be able to grow its own.

Dr Hammer telephoned the world's leading bone-marrow expert, Dr Robert Gale, who lived in Los Angeles, and said he would pay for him to fly a team out to the Soviet Union. Throughout his career, Dr Gale had been planning for such an emergency, but he never thought he would come face-to-face with such young men so brutally damaged by other people's carelessness. When Dr Gale arrived at Moscow's Hospital Number Six with bone-marrow supplies from Britain, he found many men who urgently needed a transplant. They were lying silently, barely able to communicate, in solitary rooms. Most of them were only in their twenties, their young bodies burned by radioactive dust particles. They had hacking coughs, caused by contaminated smoke particles inhaled within their sensitive lung tissue. All over the Soviet Union, village councils and city leaders were renaming roads and parks after these desperate men who had saved so many lives.

Dr Gale had spent years among cancer patients, but he felt completely overwhelmed by the scale of the firemen's suffering in the Moscow hospital. He had only a limited amount of bone marrow and just a few weeks to do what he could to help. He faced a difficult decision. Whom should he try to save? It felt uncomfortably like playing God, but he decided that he would operate on the men who had received more than 500 roentgens – the lethal radioactive dose. First he had to conduct tests to see if the men's tissues would accept the bone-marrow samples he had brought with him. If he didn't match the right men with the right samples, their bodies would reject the marrow and the transplants would be useless. His team of specialists worked fifteen hours a day. Most of the men who received the precious bone marrow have since died.

The radioactive cloud continued to disperse further north. By now it was smearing contamination across Scandinavia and much of northern Europe. The particles were blown higher and reached the jet stream. The contaminated cloud's deadly cargo was one hundred million curies of radiation. It bled across borders, carried by wind and water. It blew onto hill farms in North Wales. It rained over the fjords of Norway. It dusted the ice-flats where reindeer herds grazed in Lapland. It even interfered with the hazelnut crop in Turkey. In Belarus, it grew inside plants eaten by cattle whose meat then became radioactive.

An area the size of Great Britain was eventually so contaminated that it will be unsafe for thousands of years. Although Chernobyl is in Ukraine, most of the deadly isotopes fell on the neighbouring republic of Belarus. Radiation levels there were 100 times greater than those resulting from the nuclear bombs dropped on the Japanese cities of Hiroshima and Nagasaki during the Second World War.

Gradually, increasing numbers of evacuated children became sick with eye problems and blood disorders. Many of those who had been evacuated from Pripyat were barely able to stand up a few days later. Their skin had turned a blueish colour and they weren't hungry. When they arrived in the resettlement camps, their future was bleak. They had left behind the newly poisoned rivers, trees and gardens of their childhood and been bussed to an unfamiliar concrete landscape where they were expected to spend the rest of their lives.

The worst was yet to come, when the children's radiation levels were measured. After each reading the children were presented with different coloured labels to wear. These signified just how far the Geiger counter needle had shot around the dial. A red label was the worst kind: it meant no one could touch you. Children were suddenly outcast. More than half the children had received a dangerous dose.

Children who had been forced to abandon their homes in the deadly and deserted countryside met up with children from nearly 2,000 other towns and villages and were re-housed in soulless apartment blocks with no furniture or heating. Some of the children had been told they were leaving for only three days, but this was just a ploy to persuade them into the bus convoys. It took some parents months to find their children in the labyrinthine buildings in the new cities. When they were reunited, many families disintegrated. Husbands and wives had been forced to leave their lives behind and there was often nothing left to hold them together in this bleak, new environment. Yet those who had been resettled were the lucky ones. Many thousands of villagers couldn't be moved for years. During this time they lived as usual, eating their contaminated vegetables, milk, eggs, and meat, and becoming steadily sicker without understanding why.

More than 100,000 people have been permanently relocated from their village homes near Chernobyl to soulless high-rise flats in Minsk.

Meanwhile, sixty-five kilometres to the north of the Chernobyl reactor and just twenty-five miles from the limit of the enforced evacuation zone, the town of Bragin was among the many hundreds in turmoil. During the six months since the disaster, the 17,000 inhabitants knew that everyone inside the exclusion zone had been forcibly relocated. They also knew that their town was in the twilight zone: neither officially in the zone nor officially beyond radiation's deadly reach. Some people chose to pack up their houses and evacuate. They took what possessions they could fit on the backs of their horse-drawn carts or inside their vehicles.

Other inhabitants were reluctant to leave, particularly the farmers, and especially if they weren't being forced by the authorities to go. Some stayed, but washed down their houses with foaming buckets of hot water and soap powder just to be on the safe side. One farmer wrapped his prize cow in polythene, believing that this would protect it from radiation. He didn't realise that radioactive nuclides were entering through the animal's mouth. Most of the inhabitants felt grateful that the government hadn't told them to leave their homes, on land they knew, near their friends. They were sceptical about their neighbours' claims, and decided that the radiation rumours sweeping the village were exaggerated. It was a story repeated all over Belarus.

The Birth

Igor was born on 29 March 1987, eleven months after the Chernobyl disaster. Little is known about his parents, or about why he was signed him over to the authorities after his birth. Carefully swaddled in the traditional manner, the disabled infant with the appealing brown eyes looked like a little sausage roll with a sweet face peering out of the pastry. He stayed in the hospital where he was born for twelve days while his papers were prepared and he was legally separated from his family.

For the first eleven months of his life, Igor was shuttled from one hospital in Minsk to another, but nothing could be done for his congenital disabilities, so after a short time at Hospital Number Two he was taken to the equally imaginatively named Children's Home Number One, one of thirteen homes for young children in Minsk, where sixty-five sick and disabled boys and girls lived in seven dormitories.

The driver pulled up outside the three-story building painted in flaking red, yellow and green, and a nurse carried the baby no one appeared to want up the flight of concrete steps. Once inside, the nurse walked briskly to Dr Ludmila Kravchenko's office. She was the head doctor and could sign yet more paperwork.

The nurse rapped on the door. Ludmila's gaze was immediately drawn to the appealing bundle the nurse was holding. He was beautiful. His dark brown eyes shone. She quickly signed the papers and sat the baby on her lap. Gently, she examined him. She saw his stunted legs and felt for his right arm, finding instead the small mound. A feeling of dread washed over her. Medical training had taught her to fear radiation. Here, calmly cradled on her lap, was a little boy who was evidence of the radiation that had seeped everywhere. She felt a cold chill and hugged the baby tighter to her chest, rocking him gently back and forth and murmuring to him. It was just as she had feared. During the months after the meltdown she had thought of all the pregnant women and wondered what would happen to their unborn children.

She took Igor along the corridor, up staircases painted with gold stars and along to one of the wards painted in a soft sunflower yellow, and lay him in a cot by a vast window, drawing white cotton curtains to diffuse the sun's glare. She despaired at the enormous windows that made the building inadequate for its purpose: in summer it was always sweltering, in winter freezing. Ludmila arranged for Igor to be christened, something she did for every child who arrived in the hospital. If his natural parents couldn't care for him, God would. Despite the fact the Communist government had tried to oppress religion, people's faith continued.

Igor's cot was in a row in the centre of the dormitory. It had thin metal bars through which he could peer out at the rows and rows of cots and playpens. The dormitory was to be the only home that Igor would have for the next six years. There was to be no Mummy or Daddy, no brothers or sisters, just a dedicated staff of female nurses, and mentally and physically handicapped children. Cuddles would always be shared. Privacy would be impossible. His whole life would be acted out in the centre of the dormitory, under the bright lights and the warm scrutiny of the scurrying nurses, who worked 24 hours at a stretch and then had three days off.

Igor was a very smiley, happy baby. The nurses immediately realised that his mind was developing normally. His problems were all physical and this made him unique among the other children. He was not brain-damaged in any way and was responsive and interested in everything. His cheerful nature made him the darling of the nurses, especially Lilya Greenhouse. She had a grey curly perm, smiling grey eyes and narrow lips. Traditionally, people with thin lips in Belarus were considered unkind and ruthless, but Lilya was the opposite: very kind and gentle.

She was immediately drawn to the small child. Sometimes after lunch the nurses would set records spinning on a record player in the ward. It was one of the few ways they had to stimulate the children, hoping the gaiety of the music would provoke and excite them. Igor loved music. He was captivated by the feelings it created in his body and couldn't resist the urge to start moving. He would call out for Lilya, grabbing her hand, and she would scoop him up and dance with him, shuffling around in her low-heeled shoes and thick tights as the baby squealed with delight.

During the day, Lilya picked up Igor as often as she could. If he wasn't carried, he could only watch the other children playing from his bed and he didn't learn to toddle at the usual time because of his disability. Lilya would chatter to Igor about everything in the ward and outside in the garden. She would name objects, hoping that it might compensate for life in an institution a little, and help him to develop as normally as possible.

She would sit him down in the play area and give him a toy car to play with. Sometimes she would slip a new one out of her battered leather handbag. His eyes would shine and he would try to find out what was inside the cars. He would investigate to see if any parts opened or lifted up or disconnected. Then, when he had satisfied his inquisitive mind, he would push them hard so they sped away across the floor. Inevitably Igor was possessive of Lilya. As far as he was concerned, she was his special nurse and when she took another child out for a walk in the garden, Igor was jealous and felt angry. He would stare intently at the toy car he was playing with and concentrate all his attention on it until Lilya came back into the ward. Then, forgetting his anger, he would call out for her. When she brought him presents of sweets and biscuits, he would always give one to every child in the room.

Every day rolled past with the same regime, even Saturdays and Sundays. The children would be woken up at quarter to seven in the morning to be dressed by the nurses, although Igor always tried to put on his own clothes, thick tights and colourful jumpers. At eight o'clock those who were old enough would sit at small blue-Formica topped tables for breakfast. Wearing bibs, they would scoop up porridge, rice pudding or semolina. They would sip weak tea and eat bread and butter. The babies would be fed on powdered milk made up with water. After breakfast the children would play in yellow playpens with black rubber foam bases or be taught to draw with coloured pencils if they were able to hold them. Lunch was soup with boiled rice, pasta or mashed potatoes. Sometimes there was chicken or beef floating in the watery broth. After lunch the children would be put down to sleep for two hours. When they awoke, after taking their coats from their lockers, they could go for a walk or a pram-ride in the garden if the weather was fine. Igor was very independent and since he always liked to dress himself, his locker was closest to the dormitory. Each locker had a different hand-painted symbol stuck to its door. The children liked to pull these off and swap them around, so sometimes Igor's locker symbol was a strawberry, at other times a cherry or a flower.

If it was raining, the children would spend the afternoon inside, playing with the nurses if they had time. There was a talking parrot in a cage and goldfish in an aquarium. Igor was fascinated by everything. At four o'clock the children would be given a snack of biscuits, washed down with a cup of milk or orange juice. They would have a nap before the evening meal of porridge, semolina, rice pudding and vegetables. Then the lights were turned off at eight o'clock and there was supposed to be total hush.

Igor was usually a very obedient little boy, but when he heard Lilya tiptoeing into the ward on the evening shift after the lights had been turned off, he was unable to resist the urge to shout out her name. He knew that she would come over to hold him, and he loved to be cuddled. Each night he called to her, the other children would wake in their cots and start shouting out as well. Lilya would sigh, smile, take off her woollen coat and hang it on the brass peg, before creeping onto the ward. She would softly calm the other children down, stroking their faces and murmuring soothing words to them. Then she would walk towards Igor sitting, upright in his cot, a huge smile on his face and his eyes shining at her. As she reached him, he would stretch out his hand and catch hold of her white overalls. Lilya would cradle him, singing the Russian lullabies she had learned as a child, and Igor would then fall asleep, blissfully content.

Ludmila also loved to cuddle Igor. She felt frustrated that there was so little she could do for him. She knew that had Igor been born in the West, there would have been many treatments the surgeons could have attempted to improve his quality of life, including the possibility of operating on his legs in an attempt to turn his little feet forward. But nothing like this was possible in Belarus, where a packet of aspirins cost the equivalent of half a month's salary.

More and more damaged babies had begun arriving. Some of the new arrivals seemed quite normal on first sight, but they would turn out to have sealed ears, or thumbs that branched into two finger tips, each with a perfect nail. Before the Chernobyl disaster the dormitories had mainly been filled with children whose mothers had given them up because they were too poor to raise them. There had always been some physically and mentally handicapped children, but in the months after the nuclear disaster the number of disabled children who were being born had trebled. Some of the nurses had worked there for longer than thirty years and they were gravely concerned by the sudden increase in congenital deformities. Gradually the dormitories were filling up with profoundly damaged babies and children who were destined to spend the rest of their lives in institutions, as a shameful reminder of the Chernobyl disaster.

In February 1989, Children's Home Number One was officially turned into a specialist centre for physically disabled children. This meant that, like twelve other children's homes, it now fell under the jurisdiction of the Ministry of Health which had discovered that disorders of the central nervous system and developmental defects were increasing every year. Children were at maximum risk if they had been exposed to radiation in the womb. In April that year, Ludmila was replaced by Dr Tamara Mourashova. Tamara was a compassionate woman of thirty-one with deep blue eyes. She, too, was immediately charmed by Igor. Because his legs were so short, he seemed so tiny, but she was captivated by his intelligent gaze. "Instantly, I felt great love, compassion and pity for this child," she says.

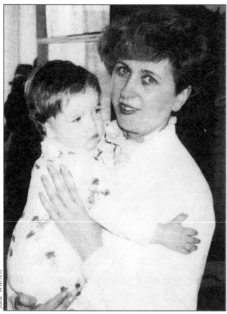

Dr Tamara Mourashova holding Nastya, another of the Chernobyl victims. Nastya was born with sealed ears, and thumbs which branched into two, each with a perfect nail.

Disabled children continued to arrive at her hospital. One day a baby whose head was three times too big was delivered, another had no arms. A little girl named Nastya had been born with sealed ears and thumbs that branched into two, each with a perfect nail. One child's legs were so badly bent and twisted that they looked like a coat hanger. Another had a severe hair lip and cleft palate – a crater that opened up the centre of his face. This defect, easily corrected in the rest of Europe, could not be dealt with here. Without treatment, such children would never learn be able to talk clearly. There were Down's Syndrome babies, and an infant with severe spina bifida had a lump the size of a fist on his back.

Tamara wondered how she could ever help them all. The government had run out of money and had stopped buying new equipment and medicines. It was difficult even to sustain life, let alone help. As more and more disabled children arrived, Tamara began to see that their existence was making her young unmarried nurses fearful of their own chances of conceiving a healthy baby. One by one, the nurses left. Tamara replaced them with older women like Lilya, who were too old to have children, or whose sons and daughters had already grown up.

Igor wasn't concerned by the physical deformities of the other children and was very gentle with them. He was so used to seeing other children with greater physical and intellectual difficulties that he never appeared to feel despair or helplessness at his own situation. Sometimes Lilya would bring Igor books with pictures of cars in them. He would concentrate intently and pick out the ones he wanted to drive when he was older. At that time, he could barely move around his cot by himself and he so longed to walk. When he was sitting on the floor, playing with the other children, he would look at their shoes. Perhaps that was the problem, he wondered? Maybe there was something wrong with his shoes. For a few weeks he kept undoing his leather buckles, kicking off his shoes, and leaning over to the other children to pull off theirs. They weren't able to complain as Igor tried to fit his feet inside in his desperate attempt to discover the secret of walking.

The Garden

When Igor was two years old, Lilya decided it was time to try to teach him to walk. There were few nurses and many children in the dormitories, so the children were normally left in their cots for much of the day. But Lilya had often taken Igor into the grassy garden at the back of the children's home. She had wanted him to spend lots of time outside in the fresh air, playing on the grass, because she could see he was unusually intelligent and alert. Each afternoon that Lilya was working at the children's home in the spring of 1989, she would settle herself outside while Igor tried to stand upright by himself, steadying himself against her body. His feet were turned out sideways, so balancing was difficult. He had never seen anyone else with a physique like his, so he had no one to copy and had to work out his own methods for standing and walking. Because his arm touched the ground, Lilya told him to lean on it. For weeks, she patiently encouraged him to use it like a third leg. Igor loved the attention she was paying him and she would always reward him with a hug that encouraged him further. He would tell every nurse and visitor to the hospital, "Lilya is teaching me to walk". He glowed with pride and practised constantly. His speech had also advanced a little. Speech usually comes at the same time as the ability to walk but, because Igor had been surrounded by children too handicapped to talk, he hadn't been immersed in normal happy chatter. When he spoke he did so very slowly and Tamara was concerned by the way he seemed to be lagging behind normal children in his vocal development.

When he was two and a half, Igor could finally walk and run. He would race up and down the ward, swinging his arm onto the ground to propel his legs forward. From that point on, when he saw Lilya or one of the other nurses pulling out the record player and selecting a record, he would race onto the linoleum floor, ready to dance. As he got older, he would excitedly turn cartwheels and spin around on one hand when the Russian folk music began. The nurses would coax the other children to join in.

Because all the nurses were female, Igor had seen few men and they were a novelty. A male driver, Misha, sometimes worked at the children's home, bringing food and driving the doctors to appointments. Igor became very friendly with Misha, partly because he was a man and partly because he was a driver and Igor loved cars. Misha was a source of fascination to all the boys in the children's home, but he took a particular shine to Igor and would sit him down on the passenger seat and let him toot the horn. Igor's fascination with cars grew stronger by the day.

Now he could walk, Lilya was able to push back the horizons of Igor's world a little further. Rather than staying in the confines of the children's home, they would walk up quiet streets shaded by avenues of trees in the south west suburbs of Minsk. Sometimes Igor would experience the ultimate thrill: a ride on a trolley bus. He loved pressing the bell to make the bus slow down, clambering down, and watching the bus rumble off without him. Then he would stand on the pavement. "Buy me that car, Lilya," he would demand, pointing at the cube-like Ladas, the most popular car in Belarus. These weren't sleek, impressive cars, but rather grumpy tin cans. To Igor, they were the most exciting things he had ever seen.

Shortly after his third birthday, Igor's kind, sweet nature appeared to be changing and he became somewhat aggressive. He would throw his toys around and push the other children. Igor had started looking in the mirror and seemed to be comparing his body with the other children's'. To their great credit, Tamara's staff immediately confronted the problem, reassuring him that his disabilities didn't make him any less important. They also told him that they believed that one day he would be helped and be given new limbs to make him look like other children.

On the 12 April 1990, Tamara phoned a research institute in Moscow to apply for artificial limbs for Igor. It looked hopeful, so Igor travelled 500 kilometres by train to meet the consultant. Unfortunately there wasn't the expertise to help him and Igor was forced to return to the children's hospital in Minsk. The nurses tried to explain the specialist's reasons, but Igor was wounded by the refusal. Tamara felt guilty that she had given him such hope, so she started taking Igor home to play with her two boys. She also made enquiries at Children's Home Number Three, to see if Igor could be transferred. The children there suffered only slight learning difficulties and Igor would have had the benefit of some schooling. She urgently wanted him to mix with normal children because his ability to structure sentences was weak, but he was refused admission because of the extent of his physical disability. The nurses there didn't think they had the time to cope with him. 'Such a child would get wet when walking in the rain because his body is so close to the pavement,' they said. Tamara responded by customising Igor a pair of waterproof trousers cut from one of her sons' wet weather gear. She could see only practical solutions, but she soon realised Children's Home Number Three didn't want Igor. This bright little boy didn't fit in anywhere: he was too intelligent for Children's Home Number One, too disabled for Number Three.

Igor's behaviour began to improve again and he shuttled around the lino floor, propelling himself with his strong arm and roaring with laughter, but he had begun to think constantly about the independence a right arm would give him. Sometimes he went to sleep thinking that if he wished hard enough one would start to grow. He would touch his shoulder and ask, 'Why haven't I got an arm here?' The nurses would explain that it just hadn't grown. There was another little boy in the ward without hands and both Igor and he were encouraged not to lose hope but to believe that one day a man would arrive who could help them. Igor seized upon this fairytale. Every time an unfamiliar man visited the children's home, Igor would become excited, catching the visitor by the trousers and demanding, "Give me an arm and give me legs". He would bombard the nurses with the same question every day: "When is the man coming who can help me". All they could say was 'one day soon'. Igor wasn't told why he had no right arm. The nurses didn't mention Chernobyl. Other than his powerful desire for an arm, Igor assumed this was how all children lived.

Lilya had been married twice, but had never had children and Igor had become the focus of her life. Her next challenge was teaching him to read. She didn't know what his future held, but she wanted to equip him to cope in the outside world should he be lucky enough ever to meet it. She found some flashcards with words printed on them. Gradually Igor learned to recognise a few letters and to copy them slowly on to pieces of paper. Igor's future was uncertain because Children's Home Number One could not be his home forever. The rules said that at four years of age the disabled children must move on to an adult institution – and rules in the Soviet Union mattered. It was hard enough to see the mentally handicapped children being taken off to a place where few people would have the time or inclination to cuddle and play with them; Tamara found it inconceivable that the authorities wanted this to be the fate of children whose only misfortune was to have been born with physical disabilities.

The adult mental institutions were located the other side of town. The children's wing was a two-storey concrete building that smelt of musty apples. Some of the windowpanes were broken and paint was flaking off the ceilings and walls. Far worse was the noise. The children inside, distressed and unloved, moaned often. Children of six and seven banged their heads against the flimsy bars in a repetitive rocking action. Staff busied themselves with ministering to the children's needs: changing sheets, feeding them soup, cleaning them up.

Tamara thought of Igor and worried desperately about his future. In such an environment as this there was no way that an intelligent and loving little boy as he would be able to thrive and develop. Worse still, was the danger that with his athletic ability and unusual deformities he might end up in a travelling circus.

Of course, Igor knew nothing about the dark threats that hung over his future. Everything in his world was contained in the warm dormitory with Tamara, the nurses and of course Lilya. Tamara picked up Igor and cuddled him. Her modest salary – the equivalent of £35 a month for a seventy-hour week – was once again overdue and she had no food in the fridge at home, but she didn't want to let Igor go. Her purse might be empty and she knew that in any other job she could walk out in protest at not being paid, but not here. She couldn't possibly abandon these children, not when she and the nurses under her instruction were all they had, even if it meant that her own children and her husband, a computer programmer, had to go without certain things. She was working nearly twelve hours a day, six days a week. She simply didn't have time to complain.

One Wednesday afternoon, Lilya decided to sit down during the dancing. Igor ran over to her. "Lilya, dance with me," he implored. "I can't do this," she said, "I'm just a tired, grey-haired old granny." Igor shook his head. "You're not a granny. You are my Lilya," and he grabbed her hand, pulled her into the centre of the room, and clung to her legs. He was only as tall as the hem on her skirt. His eyes were on a level with her knees, and how he loved to watch Lilya's knees dancing. Then one day Lilya didn't come to the Children's Home when she was supposed to. Igor waited by the door for her cheerful, smiling face all afternoon. He did the same the next day, growing ever more anxious. He missed her chunky hugs and sweet-smelling skin. Finally, one of the nurses noticed his sad expression. She sat him on her lap and said, "Lilya is ill. She's had a heart attack. Her heart is feeling better now, but she won't be able to see you while she rests." Igor felt very sad. He didn't want to play with his cars that afternoon.

Four months later, Igor was having lunch at the little table. He had a special treat of sausages on his plate. They were skating about as he tried to stab them with his fork and he wished he had another hand to help. Then he heard slow footsteps in the passage outside and looked round. The other children didn't recognise the grey-haired lady in a thick woollen coat opening the door into the room, but Igor did. He shrieked, "Lilya," slid off his chair and ran across to see her, his face brimming with excitement. Lilya wasn't well enough to work at the Children's Home after her heart attack, but she came to visit Igor whenever she could, and she would always come to the children's birthday parties. All the children with a birthday during one particular month would celebrate them together on the same day. They would dress in their best clothes, there would be poetry readings and some of the children would sing. Igor's early years were passing in a blur because one day blended into the next, but the birthday parties were memorable highlights. It was possible to look back and see a day with a difference.

Christmas was not celebrated in the former Soviet Union. Instead, New Year was the most special time of year. The nurses would prop a small pine tree in a bucket and cover it with a set of twinkling lights. Igor was mesmerized. Then, dressed in his best clothes, donated to the hospitals by German charities, he would await Father Frost whom, he hoped, would bring him a car all of his own. Unfortunately, the cars were only ever big enough to fit in his pocket.

When Igor was five, one of the younger nurses decided he needed a treat. He was such an intelligent little boy who craved new sensations. One Sunday she took him to her home in one of Minsk's micro-districts, home to many of the 50,000 resettlers from the contaminated villages. Nine-storey concrete rabbit hutches stretched in all directions. After the trolley bus had dropped them off, Igor held the nurse's hand and walked to her high-rise where her two-room apartment was located. The lift wasn't working, so he hopped up the flights of broken-tile stairs on his strong arm, swinging his legs up behind him. There were no light bulbs in the passages – they had all been stolen – so Igor had to slide his feet carefully along to make sure he didn't fall.

The nurse's apartment was another world. On the carpeted floor was an amazing cushioned seat that felt like it were hugging you when you sat in it. He hopped out of the armchair and ran to the window. Standing on another chair, he could see children playing on slides and swings down below. On the walls of the apartment was shiny flowered paper. To Igor it all seemed so comfortable. And the food served for Sunday lunch looked exotic. He stared at the fish heads and the parsley in a clear jelly and the boiled carrot, garnished with a tomato flower. There was even a pile of something that oozed bright purple paint; he had never seen steamed beetroot before.

Igor was now nearly two years older than the accepted maximum age for Tamara's children's home, and she was despairing of ever finding a place for him. Since Igor's fourth birthday, she had been telling the authorities that the tiny boy couldn't possibly be more than four. She knew she was stretching the rules, but life in an institution would be no life at all for an alert and intelligent little boy like Igor. There was also a danger that he might be hurt by the other patients, because he was so small. Tamara knew it was imperative she did all she could to could to protect the future of the little boy with the sunny disposition who had the ability to brighten the lives of everyone he met. Sometimes she lay awake at night, dreading the day the men with clipboards would find her special boy and take him away. They seemed to be so unmoved by the children whom she loved. Igor was growing up. She couldn't wait forever. But what could she do?

The Life Line

Some 1600 kilometres away, in the south of England, a fuzzy-haired, retired businessman was going for an early morning walk through his dewy fields. It was late September 1992 and Victor Mizzi was checking on his ten goats, five geese, half a dozen ducks, at least thirty chickens – all competing with each other for the title of Best Egg Layer – and thirty-five sheep with varied wool haircuts. He counted out the morning's offering of twenty-eight warm freckled eggs and strode back up the hill towards his fifteenth-century house in the stockbroker belt near Haslemere, Surrey. He heard his Swedish wife, Birgitta, shout out that coffee was ready. Victor, who was in his late fifties, had never planned to take in other people's unwanted farmyard animals. When he had sold his Maltese travel company and taken early retirement in 1985, he had intended to keep only two sheep for grass-chomping duty. But he had soon found he couldn't resist helping unwanted strays, be they feathered or furry.

He had also realised that he needed a project to keep his active mind engaged, so an advert in the local newspaper three months earlier had captured his attention. Two local women had been looking for families to give children from the area around the Chernobyl nuclear reactor a holiday. Victor, like most people, had forgotten about the disaster – it had happened over six years before, but when he had heard that there were children who still needed help, he had immediately telephoned and said that he and Birgitta would like to look after two of them. He had then read everything he could find about the plight of the children. Evacuated from their homes in the contaminated zone, he'd learned, many of them were still living on radioactive food and developing cancers that couldn't be cured due to lack of resources. Most of the children in question were from a small republic called Belarus, that used to be part of the Soviet Union before it gained independence after the fall of Communism in 1991. Although Belarus had become the most heavily contaminated area following the disaster, the government there was impoverished and couldn't do anything for the sick children.

Victor couldn't put the plight of these unknown children out of his head. Then he'd received a phone call a fortnight before the children were due to arrive to say that their holiday had been cancelled because no airline was prepared to help with free flights. Victor immediately contacted all the local people who'd also planned to host children from the same group. Within days, he'd formed a committee. Then he'd written to every house in Haslemere, pleading for their help. Two weeks later he'd raised £10,500 and his charity, Chernobyl Children Life Line, had been born.

Victor put the eggs in the fridge and sat in the kitchen with his mug of steaming coffee, opening his mail. There were many letters from people wanting to know how they could become host parents to Belarussian children. The first month-long trip had been a great success. Twenty children had visited and by the time they returned home were noticeably healthier, with glowing red cheeks, sparkling new fillings and clutching bulging holdalls stuffed with baseball caps, trainers, T-shirts, music tapes and bubble-gum – presents from their host families.

Among the mail was a large brown envelope with a German postmark, containing an article from a German newspaper. Victor smoothed out its crumpled folds and caught his breath. On the page was a black and white photograph of a tiny, naked boy, a child from Belarus. A nurse was standing behind him about to shroud him in a stripy towel. The child was disabled in a way Victor had never seen before. He had no right arm, short legs and small, turned-out feet. The article said the cause of his deformities was the dose of radiation he had received while in his mother's womb. But it was the child's face that stopped Victor in his tracks. He seemed to be staring directly out at him, with a look of such trust and helplessness. The child in the photograph was Igor.

Victor left his coffee untouched on the table and rushed to the phone. He immediately called Maria Obrasova in Belarus. Maria was part of the Belarus charity, the 26th April Foundation, which was helping to arrange the older children's visits to Britain. This time Victor had an unusual request for Maria. Could she try and locate a particular boy with short legs and only one arm? Victor knew the chances of finding him were slim, as there would be many hospitals all over the country. While he waited, he continued to arrange the monthly visits for children of between nine and sixteen to come to Britain. Just a month breathing fresh air and eating uncontaminated food was able to boost their immune system and make them healthier. But Victor couldn't forget Igor's face. Six months later, Maria rang. A Belarus newspaper had just started publishing articles about the impact of the disaster on the new generation of children. With their help she had located the boy. Victor immediately booked a flight.

Flying in low towards the airport in Minsk, he looked out of the window at the Belarussian landscape beneath him. Much of the land was undeveloped; huge pine forests lay next to desolate plains. The airport felt like a tomb. Every surface was covered in slabs of cold grey marble that was chipped at the edges. Men in green uniforms, armed with Kalashnikov rifles barked into walkie-talkies. They wore flat hats that looked like pancakes. After taking his case from the creaking luggage carousel, every item of value in Victor's luggage was logged by three men, who carefully picked through his possessions. Outside the terminal, the women watching for passengers wore bright fuschia lipstick and had bouffant, brittle hairdos. Everyone's clothes seemed a little drab and unfashionable, as if he had stepped back into the 1950s. Maria rushed forward to greet Victor warmly, and to welcome him with the traditional Slavonik greeting: a plate of salt and a loaf of bread. Salt used to be expensive and bread was the staple food, so it was a symbolic sharing of the two most precious commodities. They drove directly to the children's home, along the deserted, main road surrounded by stands of pine trees. There were hardly any cars – few people had the money to afford them. Instead they overtook many horses pulling wooden carts laden with straw.

In the children's home, Victor was introduced to Dr Tamara Mourashava, who lead him slowly through each dormitory. Everything was spotlessly clean, but wherever he looked there were cots filled with sick and badly deformed children. Tamara led him up the final flight of stairs to the dormitory that was home to the most active disabled children. At the far end was a blue table, around which four children were shovelling up vegetable soup with hunks of bread.

Igor was delighted when he heard Tamara's voice mingling with a man's. He looked around and stared intently at him. He took in Victor's fuzzy black hair and glasses, and with a big smile immediately gestured for him to come and join him. He pulled off a piece of his bread and offered it to the startled visitor. After all, Igor thought, this could be the one he had been waiting for, the man who would get him an arm and legs. Victor popped his camera on the table. Igor was fascinated, picked it up and wanted to see how every button worked.

Victor could immediately sense Igor's intelligence and felt the way his personality seemed to fill the room, obscuring his disability. He took a photo of him wearing blue dungarees that were rolled up because his legs were so short. In his arms, Igor clutched the pink and yellow teddy bear Victor had just given him. The clock was ticking round and the nurses wanted Igor to go to his cot for a nap, but he couldn't stop smiling and waving at the man.

Tamara told Victor how little money she had to help the children. Victor made no promises to the hospital, but when he arrived home he contacted the *Daily Express* newspaper in London and spoke to executive editor, Alan Frame. Alan had also visited the area near the reactor, but in Ukraine rather than Belarus, to write articles for the paper and he promised to help Victor raise some money. I was sent to meet Victor and write an article about what he had seen in the children's homes and cancer hospitals while he was in Belarus. The article was headlined 'The Inheritors of Chernobyl' and when it was published, in April 1993, hundreds of letters arrived for the charity. They contained a total of £18,000 in donations to buy medicines and to fund more visits to Britain for the older children. Companies also donated palettes of toys and clothes. One letter in particular stood out. It was written by retired army officer and former artificial limb designer, Vic Tucker, who had found himself deeply affected by the photograph of Igor, with the teddy bear, that had accompanied the article in the paper.

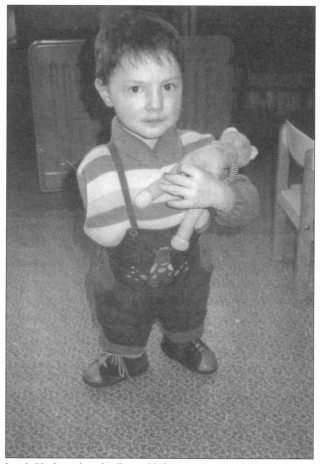

Igor holds the pink and yellow teddy bear given to him by Victor Mizzi,
this photograph was to change Igor's life forever.

arm for free if he could be brought to England for measurements and fittings. For the first time, Victor was able to contact Tamara at the children's home in Minsk to say he could help Igor. He had been hesitant to promise anything before. Two years earlier, a German charity had thought they could help the boy, but, having taken him to Germany, realised they couldn't. An Irish charity, Chernobyl Children's Project, had also filmed in the children's home and been captivated by Igor. One day, the charity's director, Adi Roche, phoned Victor to say they had met a delightful boy with only one arm, did he know him? Victor was able to tell her not only that he did but also that Igor was coming to Britain. Adi responded by sending a £500 donation to help.

The plan was to bring Igor to England for six months for the design and fitting of the new limb. But the boy would need somewhere to live. Victor was looking for someone very experienced. Caring for Igor would be a huge responsibility. He needed to find someone who could make a decision with their head as well as their heart, he didn't want Igor to end up like an abandoned puppy after Christmas. The obvious choice was Barbara Bennett, whom Victor had met after she too had advertised for people to host children from Chernobyl. He had contacted her to say he was doing the same thing, and they had joined forces and become friends. Victor knew she would see the boy, not his disability.

One of the many photographs of Igor playing with the fire engine given to Igor by former artificial limb designer, Vic Tucker

Barbara had been a foster carer for nearly thirty years. She and her husband, Roy, have five children and many grandchildren of their own, and have fostered more than a hundred children, including their foster daughter Sarah who arrived when she was ten months old for a six week stay that lasted 16 years. There have always been at least two children staying at any one time at their house in Farncombe, Surrey. If you count short stays and holiday-placement schemes, over 250 children had been able to call the Bennett's house home.

Victor's request was a big decision for Barbara. She had never fostered a child as disabled as Igor, and the language barrier was another complicating factor to consider. Would Igor be able to adapt to her busy regime? She was also a registered child-minder, so the house was often overflowing with demanding pre-schoolers aged from six months to five years during school hours, and older children afterwards. She also knew it was vital for Igor to feel comfortable with her. She needed to meet him. When she flew with Victor to Minsk one weekend in October 1993, Barbara still felt totally unsure. Since the break-up of the Soviet Union, of which Belarus had been just a tiny part, people had little money. It was difficult to find any food to buy. As Barbara looked out of the window, as they drove through Minsk, she could see queues of people standing in front of small kiosks on the edges of the pavements, hoping to purchase whatever supplies the shopkeeper had been able to source. One day it might be bananas or potatoes, another day cigarette lighters or razor-blades.

They parked outside the children's home and Barbara was struck by how much the outside looked like a concrete warehouse. She didn't know what to expect, but inside the walls were covered with murals of countryside scenes, the floors were spotlessly clean and the air was filled with a sweet scent. Tamara explained that Igor was outside with the nurses in the garden and she and Victor discussed the details of the plan to bring Igor to Britain for treatment. Next, Tamara and Barbara chatted informally over coffee and Belarussian cakes with the help of a translator.

"We have a big family with lots of grandchildren," said Barbara. "I look after other children as well."

Victor added, "In some ways it will only be a slight change for Igor, he won't be plucked out of his dormitory and into isolation."

Tamara was relieved to meet the woman Victor had chosen to give Igor a secure home for the months he would be away. "Barbara was in her early fifties, older than I had expected, and that reassured me," said Tamara. She then showed her visitors around the children's dormitories. She pointed out Igor's cot just before he loped back into the ward. Dressed in a peaked cap and wearing a big brown woollen coat, he looked like a little sparrow. Igor saw Victor and let out a yelp of delight. He raced over and wrapped his left arm around him. This was the man whom Tamara had said was the one who was going to give him an arm and make his dreams of being a fire fighter come true.

The man had many bags with him. Perhaps the arm was hiding inside, holding something in its fingertips. Igor undid the zips and buckles and felt around. "Where is the arm?" he kept saying in Russian. It was the first time Victor had heard him speak. All Igor could find were cuddly toys, which would be lovely to play with later, but at the moment he had a mission. Then Igor saw a lady who looked a bit like Lilya crouching down next to the man and smiling at him. It was Barbara. Hanging over the lady's shoulder was another, smaller bag ... the arm must be inside that. Igor ran over and the lady let him open her handbag. Anxiously he peered inside, but there was no arm. He spoke to Victor and Barbara's translator briskly in Russian.

"I need the arm. I'm being told off because I can't wash behind my ears properly, and with two arms I'll be able to put the fire engine on another shelf. Someone keeps taking it down."

Tamara explained to Victor that Igor thought he was going to get a real arm. Then she looked at Igor and said, "Victor couldn't bring the arm with him. You can go to England with his friend, Barbara, if you like. She will look after you and then they will make you a special arm."

Igor desperately wanted to go, but it didn't seem fair. He thought for a moment and said in his loud, commanding voice, "I've already been away to Germany. Someone else should go."

Barbara studied this angelic little boy chattering away in a confident, loud, deep voice. "He was so bright, it was almost as if he shone," she says. He had lovely curly hair and a mischievous grin on his face. Although his face was that of a six year old, he was still dressed like a baby in little woollen tights. He looked lost. Barbara just knew he had to come and stay with her; he needed the love of a family. She wanted to do everything she could to help him. Because the arrangement was to last only six months, she decided to tackle any problems as they arose. Igor was small, just over sixty centimetres tall, but his personality more than compensated for his short stature. He had a functioning body that was just different to everyone else's. From her trip around the children's home, and from a previous visit to Minsk, she knew there were other child victims of Chernobyl who were much worse off. After an hour it was time to leave. It was to be three months until Barbara would see Igor again.

Once he was home, Victor contacted Alan Frame at the *Daily Express*. He wanted to book Igor on to a flight to Britain three days after Christmas. The plan was for the boy to receive three months of physiotherapy at Queen Mary's Hospital in Roehampton to prepare him to receive the new arm. But Victor needed to raise some more money to pay for Igor's living expenses for six months and to put some in reserve for his future. He planned to find a way to give Igor a more secure long-term future. Without funding, Igor might have to return home to the children's home, where the threat of being forced to move to a mental institution still hovered. Sufficient charitable donations could allow him to go to school in Minsk, or perhaps pay for a future with a Belarussian family who could adopt him. Victor knew Igor was an extraordinary child who deserved to have hopes for the future like any little boy. He hoped another newspaper article specifically aimed at raising money for Igor's rescue would give him that chance.

The second article I wrote about Igor was called 'Igor's Fight For a Future'. Published on 11 November 1993, it was illustrated with the proud picture of Igor clutching the fire engine Vic Tucker had given him. It explained Igor's hopes for a new arm to help him put his fire engine on a higher shelf, and on a more poignant note outlined the future he would inevitably face if the Charity couldn't help him. The response to the article was breathtaking. Haslemere post office was jammed with letters arriving at the rate of 300 a day. The postman had to deliver them in giant cloth sacks. In the first week alone, Victor received donations totalling £15,000 for Igor and other children like him in Belarus. His phone rang constantly as he embarked on the mammoth task of replying personally to each letter. Victor then carefully folded each one back into its envelope and filed them all away in boxes. He wanted Igor to have a record of all the people who had given him a future.

Some of the letters were typed on company writing paper; others were written in biro on notepaper, or on pieces of lined paper torn from exercise books. Many of the letters were very touching.

Our seven-year-old son died a year and half ago of a rare disease and there is still £500 left in the fund raised by local people. We would like to give the money to your cause for Igor.

Alison Sneath, Dartford, Kent.

I was so moved by Igor's spirit, in spite of all his difficulties, that I felt I must do something to help. Each spring I sow a few seeds such as tomatoes, cucumbers and a few herbs. I always grow more than I need for myself. This year I decided to see if I could sell the leftovers to friends and workmates for a nominal charge. The proceeds from this sale come to £7, for which I have enclosed my cheque. I know it is not a lot, but I am of the opinion that every little helps. I hope you agree.

Mr Wiles, Tunbridge Wells, Kent.

I enclose a cheque and hope your appeal will touch many hearts.

John Watson, Bournemouth, Dorset.

After reading about Igor I have raised £49.62 from a sponsored swimming event.

Paul Spinks, Frinton-on-Sea, Essex.

When you published Igor's photograph a few months ago I cut it out and cried every time I looked at it. ˅

Mrs Nairn Bradford, Yorkshire.

Some donations were accompanied by unsigned jottings of goodwill. £10 and £20 notes fell out of some envelopes containing no note at all. One small scrap of paper simply said in pencil, 'From an 86-year old age pensioner'. A sheet of cream writing paper bore the words, 'This donation is in memory of my aunt, who died recently, and would have wanted to help.' Someone else had written, 'I am on income support and I consider it a privilege to be able to help this beautiful, intelligent little boy in some way.'

Igor had been given a future.

58 DAILY EXPRESS Thursday November 11 1993

Igor's fight for a future

Sad victim of radiation hell needs our help

DAILY EXPRESS

CHILDREN OF CHERNOBYL APPEAL

By JANE WARREN

H E is a forgotten child of Chernobyl. Now aged seven, Igor Pavlovec had just been conceived when the nuclear reactor exploded in 1986 just 140 miles south of his home.

His mother didn't realise the significance of the disaster — or the impact it would have upon her unborn baby — and refused to leave the area.

Igor was the first child to be born after the melt-down. His tiny body bears the cruel legacy of radiation. The size of a baby, his feet are turned out in a permanent fishtail and he has just one arm.

But his mind is sound and, although aware of his appalling deformities, he keeps smiling. His cheerful spirit has made him the darling of the nurses who care for him.

When Igor was born, his mother was ashamed at the genetic defects radiation had wrought on her child. She cut herself from radiation sickness and without the money to cope, she gave her baby to the nurses and turned quietly away.

The nurses named him Igor and placed him in a hospital orphanage in Minsk, 45 miles north of Chernobyl, in the state of Belarus.

But the ward Igor has considered home all his life is full. Wall-to-wall with tiny cots, there are new babies being born with deformities every day. Experts predict that cases of child cancer per cent will continue to increase until at least 1997.

A ruling says that when a child is seven years old, he must move on from the hospital orphanage to an adult asylum. Igor should have been moved several months ago but remains because the doctors on the ward are fighting to stop him leaving.

Fundraiser Victor Mizzi, who took this photograph of Igor, explains that if the boy is moved it will be a tragedy.

"Igor is a very intelligent. If he goes to an adult institution, he will be swallowed up into the system. He is extremely bright and his personality fills the room."

Victor is chairman of Chernobyl Children Life Line, which helps children suffering with radiation diseases in conjunction with a Belarus-based charity.

"Igor has no illusions about his condition but craves for the independence an artificial arm will give him," he says. *"Belarus state has no interest in helping Igor, they are covering up the plight of these damaged children.*

In a short-term bid to help Igor, Victor has booked him on a flight to Britain three days after Christmas. He will receive three months of physiotherapy to prepare him for the new arm.

Victor is still trying to raise enough money to provide it.

"Igor thinks about nothing but his arm," says Victor. *"When I visited his hospital, he kept asking if I was coming back. He need to wash behind my ear.' He is very excited that one day soon he might be able to play properly with his fire engine."*

T HE bright red toy engine is Igor's most treasured possession. It was given to him by a Daily Express reader who read our article six months ago about the children damaged by radiation.

Following that feature, the kindness of Express readers raised £18,000 for the child victims of the world's worst industrial accident.

Igor places the engine on a shelf above his bed but other children keep taking it down," says Victor. *"He is convinced that if he has another arm, he will be able to keep it safe."*

But artificial limb technology is expensive. The charity needs your donations.

And there is another, more pressing concern. After the fitting has gone ahead, Igor will return home to an adult institution . . . unless we can raise enough to send him to a school in Britain and then a family who would like to adopt him.

Victor says: *"Igor is an extraordinary individual. He deserves to have hopes for the future like any little boy. Your donations will give him that chance."*

● Money and air miles should be sent to: Igor Fund, Chernobyl Children Life Line, Courts, 61 Petworth Road. Haslemere, Surrey GU27 3AX. Cheques should be made payable to: Chernobyl Children Life Line.

● Readers interested in forming a Life Line link to raise funds to bring 10 children and one adult to Britain for a holiday — which will provide a valuable respite from the radioactive environment — can write to Victor Mizzi at the above address.

PRECIOUS: Igor hugs his treasured toy

The Escape

Lilya and Igor spent a happy last afternoon together before he flew to London. They played with his fire engine and walked in the garden of the children's home. Although Lilya had been told Igor would only be away for six months, she knew she wouldn't see him again for a very long time. No one who set eyes on Igor could ever let him go. Then it was time to say goodbye. Lilya decided not to go to the airport with Tamara, who was flying to England to help Igor settle in. She couldn't trust her emotions. So she picked him up and gave him a good hug. Then she kissed his forehead. He was giggling and smiling, and wanted her to kiss him on the lips. Tears threatened, but she forced them back. Igor mustn't see how sad she was. She must only show him the part of her that was pleased for him. Igor was excited and anxious in equal measure before he left for England and his sleep was fitful.

Igor arrived at Heathrow on 4 January 1994. The four-hour flight had alarmed him, especially when Tamara had explained they would be flying over the sea. "What if the plane falls into the water. I don't have legs to swim," Igor had said, clutching his seat. But the air stewardesses, with their ritual of serving food from rattling metal trolleys squeezing up and down the aisle had fascinated him. Tamara wheeled him into the arrivals hall in an airport wheelchair. Cocooned in a fluffy blue woollen coat, he was dwarfed by the bicycle-size wheels. His eyes were wide with excitement. He'd rarely been in a wheelchair before, so it was quite an adventure. A television crew shone their lights and pointed their big black camera and fuzzy sound-boom at him. "Thank you. Thank you," he said in English, words that Tamara had taught him on the plane. Barbara gave him a hug and Victor popped a red Christmas hat with a white bobble on his head. There was a press conference at the airport, but Igor was more interested in the toy car Victor had given him than in the cameras. As Victor answered questions, Igor investigated. He opened the bonnet and examined the engine, oblivious to the flashing cameras.

It was nearly midnight when they reached Farncombe, an hour's drive from the airport. Barbara carried Igor upstairs to the first bedroom he had ever known where there was a special surprise waiting for the little boy who was used only to the stark, anonymous surroundings of a hospital ward: his own racing-car bed. Bright green, it even had a hand painted number plate that bore his name. There were also mobiles, a coloured patchwork clown and shelves of cuddly toys. Every time Igor looked at the bed, he could hardly believe what he was seeing. He had found himself in a new and enchanting world where people even *slept* in vehicles.

Barbara showed Tamara to her room and watched as she unpacked Igor's bag. A few pairs of tights, a couple of pairs of pants and some socks were his only possessions. He had no other toys or books. The bright red fire engine had been left behind with the other children, because the nurses thought he would be back soon. The next day Barbara put on a vivid crimson satin shirt, and drove Igor to Victor's house to meet the ITV and SKY television crews. Igor was fascinated by the twenty-minute journey to Haslemere. The fields, shops, houses and sign-posts all intrigued him, while the speed of the cars on the A286 was exhilarating. But danger lurked inside Victor's house. A large black wolf sat in the hall. Igor was terrified by the colossal woolly creature, who was bigger than he was. He had never touched a dog before and grabbed hold of Tamara for reassurance. "This is Rip," said Victor, "He is a very gentle dog". Igor regarded the black furry mountain. Rip regarded him. Then the eight-year old Labrador/ wolf-hound ambled over and lay down in front of him. Igor was nervous, but he carefully reached out his hand and touched the dog's soft tummy. The canine giant breathed softly.

Victor scooped Igor up and sat him on a sofa covered in Christmas packages and the hundreds of letters that had arrived for him. Igor's keen eyes were interested in everything around him: the ringing telephone, the television cameras, the parcels. He talked rapidly in his strong, confident voice as the cameras filmed him. "When I grow up I'm going to drive a car and I'm going to drive it so fast that none of your policeman will be able to catch me," he said earnestly in Russian. He slapped his leg to call Rip over for a biscuit, then he jumped off the sofa, and shuttled up and down the room so fast in his excitement that the cameramen had to ask him to slow down so they could film him. He was fascinated by Victor's collection of over 200 ornamental owls arranged on shelves that reached from floor to ceiling. There were wooden ones, fluffy ones and ceramic ones. Some had clock-faces that ticked. Igor turned cartwheels on the cream-coloured carpet.

A few days later it was time for Igor to go to Queen Mary's Hospital in Roehampton for the first appointment to see about his bionic arm. He was accompanied by Victor, Barbara, Tamara, and Vic Tucker. Many boys of six are preoccupied by soccer and video games. They race down the football pitch or coordinate the controls of their hand-held computer games with ease. They take mobility and dexterity for granted. Igor longed to experience such freedom, but he was equally excited by the prospect of being able to wash his own face properly or tie his own shoelaces.

Hugh Steeper Ltd has been Britain's leading artificial limb-makers for more than eighty years. The company has supplied prosthetics to thousands of people worldwide, including the victims of both world wars, as well as the Falklands, Gulf and Northern Irish conflicts. They have thirty branches in the UK and four overseas, and are the only upper-limb manufacturers in Britain. Their main unit is a single-storey building at Queen Mary's, where a maze of fitting rooms and offices snakes along a passage that leads to the workshop. Igor peered into the open doors as Barbara tried to coax him along, and he couldn't believe what he was seeing. Inside each room were perfect hands, legs, arms and feet. Some of them were resting on tables, others were mounted on the wall or stacked on shelves.

Igor said hello to Bob Taylor, the managing director of Steeper's who had agreed to treat him for free when he had heard about his plight from Vic Tucker. Then he met the consultant in rehabilitation medicine, Dr Sellaiah Sooriakumaram, who picked him up and gently popped him down on a paper-covered bed topped with a blue towel. "Let's have a look at you, shall we, young man," he said. Igor knew that Dr Soori, as he preferred to call himself, and his colleagues were the men he had dreamed about, the men who would be able to give him a perfect right hand to match his left.

Igor was wearing a T-shirt with a picture of a grinning frog on it. Dr Soori took hold of his strong left arm and Igor sat patiently while he flexed it and experimented with other parts of his body. Then the doctor took Igor's socks off and examined his feet. Igor was ticklish and he giggled. A lot of discussions were taking place about how best to help him, but even though he couldn't understand a word, he was perfectly behaved. He knew it was the only way to be if he wanted a new arm. Everyone was very impressed with his spirited good humour. Dr Soori discovered that even though Igor was nearly seven, he was the height of an average two-year old, seventy-six centimetres (2ft 6"), while most children his age were between 105 and 120 cm (3ft 5" and 3ft 11") tall.

Tamara had told Igor that his new arm would be covered with lifelike plastic skin, which to Igor sounded as if he was going to get a real limb. The doctor explained to Victor in fact the bionic arm would have to be a fairly basic design, but Igor didn't understand anything these adults were saying as they discussed his future. He started dreaming again about all the things he would be able to do with two arms.

"Our experience with children who have complex underdeveloped limbs is that they do best initially if their new arm is mechanically simple," said the doctor.

Igor was already dreaming of being able to scale Barbara's climbing frame to reach the top without help. Then his imagination took him up amongst the uppermost branches of the ancient oak near Barbara's house. Finally he saw himself perched at the dizzy top of a fireman's ladder, seizing a helpless child with his powerful arms and carrying her back down through the smoke to safety.

"If they are provided with too many functions to control, the arm becomes too complicated to operate," finished Dr Soori. Then Dr Soori showed Igor the type of arm that Steeper's would build him. Igor's eyebrows knotted and his smile seemed to fade. He pulled Tamara's sleeve and whispered in her ear. "He thought he was going to get a real arm ... like his other one," she said. But he soon cheered up. He seized it and shook hands with it. And he was quick to point out that the arm he was being shown was a left arm – and he already had one of those.

Igor draws himself with two arms and two legs

He put his hand inside the closed bionic fingers, before examining it minutely from every angle. He tried to put the arm on, but it was much too large and didn't fit his shoulder, so instead he worked the buttons that were positioned near the shoulder. They opened and closed the fingers of the 'Scamp' hand, that Steeper's have been responsible for developing. Igor smiled with excitement and put his ear next to the servo-motors to hear them humming as the fingers moved.

Igor was then X-rayed. Afterwards, Dr Soori had good news. "Igor can definitely make good use of a bionic arm. And we think we might be able to do something for his legs." Igor could propel himself forward by rocking from one foot to the other and pushing himself along with his arm. It was a surprisingly efficient way of getting around and he could build up considerable speed. The action looked effortless as he gambolled away, a huge smile on his face. But from a medical point of view Igor's unusual legs were the biggest problem. The doctors at Steeper's had seen legs like Igor's before, in the 1960s and 1970s, when they had treated Thalidomide children, whose disabilities were caused by an anti-nausea drug prescribed to their mothers in early pregnancy that proved to have devastating side-effects. The babies were sometimes born with malformed flipper-like feet and short arms.

Steeper's decided on a simple approach to begin with. They planned to design a pair of special platform boots that would increase Igor's height by 13cm as well as distributing the load more evenly across his feet as he was currently walking on the back of his heels. Igor was very mobile and they didn't want the shoes to hinder his ability, but Dr Soori thought that Igor would benefit from being a few centimetres taller, the question was just how high the platform soles could be without becoming a hindrance? When the specialists had seen how Igor coped with the first pair, and after he had grown a little more, they would have a clearer idea about more advanced options for the future. Dr Soori urged Victor to apply to extend Igor's stay in Britain. "The boots will take longer than six months to design. We are so impressed with him that we want to help him. Is it possible to extend his visa indefinitely?" It was just as Igor's nurse Lilya had predicted. Victor said he would talk to the Home Office and see what could be done. More appointments were booked before Igor was driven home, waving at the prosthetic specialists in their white lab coats.

After only a week in Britain, Igor was adapting well to life outside the hospital ward in Minsk. He was fascinated by shopping in Sainsbury's in Godalming and insisted on loading the trolley with kiwi fruit and melons. Food was a source of great fascination for Igor, a fact that pleased Barbara, as she was keen to feed him up with nourishing, vitamin-rich meals. Igor was amazed at the amount of fresh milk available in the supermarket. In the children's home, milk had always been a great luxury, as were eggs and butter. Igor had rarely seen fresh fruit and vegetables, so he would stare at the fruit bowl on Barbara's kitchen table, mesmerised by the different shapes and colours. He had eaten only apples in Minsk, and just once a month if he was lucky. Barbara discovered that Igor particularly liked grapes, his face would light up when she gave him a bunch; she said it felt as if she was giving him the world. Igor's mind was experiencing all these new flavours, textures and smells at the same rate as his tummy was filling up with fresh food. For his first Sunday lunch, Barbara served roast chicken with roast potatoes and all the trimmings. Igor was hypnotised by the sight of a plate with so much food on it. He kept offering his plate round. "In the dormitory everything is shared," Tamara explained.

Barbara would give Igor the same food as the rest of the family and Tamara, but Igor wouldn't pick up a knife or fork, as he was so used to eating with a spoon, and for the first few weeks, he would hesitate before deciding what to eat. Breakfast was the most challenging meal of the day. Igor had never seen ready-sliced bread, yoghurts or cereals, and he wasn't particularly keen on the crunching sensation of Cornflakes and Rice Crispies. Each morning Barbara would pour him a little bowl from a different packet as a test, making a mental note of the ones he seemed to like. His favourite foods, beside fruit, were pork sausages and fish. Igor wasn't used to sleeping in a room by himself, so Barbara moved Tamara's bed into Igor's room, next to his racing car bed. Every night, he asked Tamara to kiss him goodnight and to bless him. Igor would then say, "God bless me in my sleep". Gradually Tamara began to prepare Igor for her departure. She told him that she would be leaving, but he would be well looked after by these kind people. Igor felt very secure in Barbara's home and he knew Victor cared for him as well. He was the man who had been able to make his dreams come true. He felt full of hope for the new limbs he had been promised.

Igor's comment to the television cameras, when he first arrived in Britain, about wanting to drive a fast car had been translated into English when the news bulletin was broadcast and had inspired viewers' generosity. Within a week he had received several remote-control cars and he quickly learned to operate the joystick efficiently with his one hand. He would then spend hours thoroughly absorbed with a car that didn't need pushing along the floor. Among the letters Victor received was one from two sisters aged seven and nine. They wrote, 'We have saved our sweets' money. Please use this for Igor and children like him'. Sixty pence in coins was jingling about at the bottom of the envelope.

A week later, Igor made his second trip to Queen Mary's Hospital. Alan Stephenson was the prosthetist orthotist who would design the bionic arm. Igor liked this tall man with floppy hair immediately. He had to take a plaster-cast impression of Igor's shoulder, so the boy took off his T-shirt and Alan wrapped his small body in green paper to stop him getting covered in Plaster of Paris. Igor had to concentrate. He needed to keep still, but the drips of water were chilly. He knew that after the plaster-cast fitting, he must be patient and wait for the arm to be made. Alan's first job would be to design the platform boots in order to determine the length of the new arm, so he measured Igor's feet as well. He was delighted with the boy's interest in the different processes.

Tamara had planned to stay four to six weeks in Britain. But one morning, nearly three weeks after she had arrived with Igor, there was an urgent phone call from the children's hospital in Minsk. An urgent funding meeting had been called by the local government and she had to go back to argue her case for a bigger budget. Within forty-eight hours she was gone, but before she left she gave full authority for Igor's welfare to Victor, on behalf of Belarus. In a document signed by the Belarus consul in London, Victor took responsibility for overseeing Igor's medical treatment and looking after his interests in Britain.

It was only after Tamara had left that Barbara bathed him for the first time. Until then she had never seen him naked. He was initially shy about his body, but Barbara reassured him, carefully bathed him, and hid the tights that he had been wearing away. She dressed him in underpants, shorts and socks. It was an important moment. Igor was still like an overgrown baby in so many ways. The next few months would see him develop into a boy. Barbara wanted to give him the opportunity to become independent and develop his already vibrant personality. She always made sure Igor was dressed before the other children she looked after arrived each morning and she never undressed him until they had gone. She wanted them to see Igor, not his deformities. Igor loved the company of the other children. He was stimulated by their responsive chatter, joined in from the first day and asked what all the toys were called. A little girl named Kirsty made a particular impression. Like the nurse's daughter at the children's home in Minsk, she had fair hair. She would let him brush it, and he found this comforting. Barbara thought Igor might be unsettled without Tamara, but he didn't appear obviously to miss her after she left. He was safe, warm and well fed. Most importantly, he had a racing-car bed and a fleet of electric cars to control. The thought of the metal cot in the dormitory was no match for all that. And perhaps he sensed that ignoring the past would give him the best possible chance of remaining in this new, exciting present. If he pined for his former life, someone might feel a temptation to return him to it. Soon he had managed to almost completely forget his life in the children's hospital.

Back at Queen Mary's for his third visit, Alan explained to Igor that he planned to give him an arm made of lightweight plastic. It would enable him to hold his cutlery and toys. Alan knew Igor would find life much easier if he could grasp things. It would allow him to keep a firm grip while his strong left hand moved them around. He would be able to seize a tube of toothpaste in his bionic arm and gently unscrew the cap using his own fingers. He would be able to clutch a felt-tip pen in his new hand and pull off the lid with his natural hand. But Alan faced considerable challenges if he were to give Igor the highly-responsive arm he craved. Artificial-limb technology is a complex enough procedure, but the potential problems and difficulties in design multiply with every additional joint requiring replacement. Igor needed not just a hand, but a wrist and an elbow too. Alan explained that the arm would be fitted with an electronic hand to allow the fingers gently to open and close. "You will have to learn to move your shoulder just the right amount, and in the correct direction, to make the fingers obey your instructions."

Igor couldn't wait. He was brimming with excitement.

The Arm

A special bond between the Belarussian child and his English Foster Mother had begun to develop. Barbara understood only a few words of Russian and had no time to learn. She needed Igor to learn English, so she treated him as if he didn't talk at all. They began to communicate by sign language and drawing pictures. If they were going for a walk, she would walk her fingers along the table top during breakfast. If she drove him somewhere, she would say 'machina' – which means 'car' in Russian. To prepare him for where they were going or what they were about to do, she would do a drawing. If it was to be a trip to the beach, fifty kilometres away on the south coast, her drawing would show the sea with a sailing boat bobbing about on crested waves. From her sketches, Igor would know which clothes to wear. If it was to be a visit to the park, she would sketch trees, a duck and a pond. Igor particularly enjoyed the ducks. He loved to watch them swimming freely on the pond. He hadn't known such birds could be wild, having only ever seen a rather depressed parrot in a cage in the children's hospital.

Barbara took Igor everywhere with her, chattering away to him constantly so he could familiarise himself with the sound of the English language. She was amazed by how quickly he started picking up words and how much of her conversation he seemed able to understand after only a few months. She taught him to count, using her fingers to reach up to ten. But Igor joked he could only count to five, because he had only one hand. As Igor was only 'borrowed', Barbara wanted to have as much fun with him as possible. Even going out in public was a treat. Because of all the publicity about Igor's arrival in Farncombe, Barbara found that rather than staring at him, people were coming up and saying, 'Hello Igor'. No one treated him as an oddity or stared unkindly at him. Instead, he swiftly became a local celebrity. In the Post Office Barbara would lift him up to stand on the counter and tell him how many stamps to ask for. He would mimic her sounds in his gruff Soviet/Surrey accent and smile at the lady behind the glass barrier. He would help Barbara to stick the stamps on envelopes and she would carry him so he could post them in the pillar-box. He didn't appear phased by any of these new experiences.

Barbara would watch him charging around her house, using his arm for balance. He was so active and independent that at times she found herself forgetting his disability. She certainly had to do nothing more for him than for any other seven year old. Although his eyes were permanently out on stalks, nothing seemed to be too much for him. He certainly didn't let his disabilities stop him doing anything he wanted. Barbara also loved his innocence; he was so rewarding. She gave him a bright red balloon on a string one day and he gazed at it for ages in wonderment – he'd never seen such a thing before. She adored the way he poured enthusiasm into everything.

After only a month in Britain, Igor was already speaking whole sentences in English. He was fascinated by every step towards an arm. During the next of his weekly visits to Queen Mary's, Alan placed a plastic cap made from the plaster-cast impression on Igor's shoulder. "That's a pretty good fit," he said proudly and marked the cap with a chalk line where it would have to be cut. By now a television crew was regularly filming Igor's quest for his new arm. Victor Mizzi had always felt there was a story to be told about the courage of Igor. Through an acquaintance, he had been introduced to the production company Zeneth Entertainment, which wanted to make a documentary about his early life and journey to the West. They had started filming scenes at Barbara's home, in the park and at the hospital.

Two months after Igor arrived in Britain, Victor had good news. The Home Office had agreed to grant an extension on Igor's visa. He could stay in England until 25 February 1996 – another two years. It was now important for Victor's legal relationship with Igor to be properly defined. When Tamara left the UK no one in Britain had legal responsibility for Igor's welfare, so Victor applied to the High Court in London to make him a Ward of Court. This meant that Igor would be beyond the jurisdiction of Belarussian politics, with the Wardship Court overseeing all decisions about his welfare. The British court order gave Victor Care and Control of Igor. Barbara Bennett was paid to be his Foster Mother by the Charity, Chernobyl Children Life Line, and she also received Disability Allowance and Child Allowance for Igor, "Although the love and care and time she gives Igor outstrips any financial consideration," says Victor. Until his 18th birthday, it would be the Official Solicitor's job to represent Igor. Social services were also involved in arranging quarterly meetings with Barbara, Victor, a representative from Igor's school, and other interested parties

When Igor first arrived, Barbara started compiling his life-story book. This was a scrapbook she began for each child she fostered to give some continuity to their life. Igor's contained newspaper articles about the Chernobyl disaster and his discovery by Victor Mizzi, stuck alongside some of his first drawings. But as the bond between Igor and Barbara developed, her commitment to the book waned. She had already begun to hope that he would never leave. Barbara told Igor that soon he would have a birthday. He didn't seem to know quite what this entailed, so she spent an hour explaining that when he went to bed he would be six, but when he woke up he would be seven. She also told him that he would have a birthday party on the great day itself. The children Barbara cared for brought Igor presents, including a fireman's bucket and another fire engine. There were plates of crisps and sandwiches, and he was bewitched by the cake with seven burning candles that Barbara placed in front of him. He blew as hard as he could as the other children clapped and laughed. They played games and danced around with balloons, but at the end of the party, as the children were leaving, Igor started handing his presents back. Barbara explained they were his to keep and he proudly carried them upstairs to his bedroom as if they were diamonds.

At the end of March Igor went to Queen Mary's again, this time to be laced into his new, elevated orthopaedic boots. They looked a bit like way-out platform shoes from the 1960s. Made from shiny black leather, they had a thick wedge heel of cork and a rubber sole. Although they were light, they did look rather solid, but Alan Stephenson explained they were just a prototype. They were laced on to Igor's feet and he was placed next to a walking *barre* – two adjustable low poles that stretched the length of the consulting room. Igor felt his short legs buckling beneath him and he adjusted his weight so he could stand upright. He made a tentative step, holding onto the *barre*, but felt he was tipping backwards. He leaned further forward and slowly hobbled along, grasping the *barre* for support. After a number of tense trips back and forth, he dared to take his hand off the *barre* and made several quick steps by himself. Barbara crouched down and held out her arms at the end of the *barre*. Igor teetered for the final few steps and melted into a grateful hug in her arms. She was bursting with pride and admiration.

Barbara was a little alarmed by the boots, though, because for the first time Igor looked as if he was disabled. She was worried people might now pity him. But Igor seemed grateful for the extra height; he was now tall enough to see inside the kitchen drawer and out of the windows. "I like being bigger," he announced one day. After a few weeks of wearing them all day long, he had mastered his balance and could walk without a wobble, although he was unable to move as fast as before. He learned to kick a football with the flat side of the boot, and once kicked so hard that the ball flew into the air and smashed a window in Roy's garden shed. Igor was open-mouthed at the sound of breaking glass, but was secretly rather elated at his ability to create such drama with his solid new boots. He liked to wash them and carefully buff them up to a shine worthy of a chief fireman; within a few weeks, he had used up three tins of shoe-polish. The boots also allowed him to ride his sturdy push-car. Igor could confidently propel himself along and then lift them off the ground like wings as he coasted down inclines in the pavement outside Barbara's house. He felt powerful and fearless. He would swing his legs off the push-car and stride around. Unfortunately, within a few weeks, the left boot began to feel tight. The larger of his two left toes was growing disproportionately fast compared to the other one. "Cut if off, cut it off. Have you got big scissors?" he begged Barbara. Wisely, she hid all the scissors in the house in case Igor's frustration and reputation for getting his own way combined, with painful results.

Igor had settled into British life remarkably well, but there were still occasional signs of his early life in an institution. His sense of tidiness bordered on the fanatical. One day Barbara hurriedly stuffed some of his underwear into his drawer, the next time she looked it had all been neatly folded into piles and smoothed flat. Barbara also noticed that if she put one of Igor's toys back in a different place, he would move it to exactly the position it had been in before. Pens, pencils, elastic bands and envelopes were going missing. She knew Igor had them, but when she questioned him he responded with a mischievous grin. She assumed that because he had never owned anything, he thought he had to hide things to prevent them being taken away.

Igor relished the opportunities and excitement offered by his new life, but right from the beginning he was frightened of being returned to his dormitory in the children's hospital. He decided that there was only one way he could stop this happening. He would refuse to speak Russian. He wouldn't talk to the parties of Belarussian children who visited Victor or Barbara for a month's holiday under the Chernobyl Children Life Line scheme. The adults accompanying the groups made great efforts to talk to him, but Igor remained silent and sullen. The language reminded him of an early existence he preferred to forget. Barbara was aware that continuity was important. Once his English began to develop sufficiently well, she would ask him about life in the children's hospital but Igor was reluctant to talk and told Barbara very little of his life in Minsk. Sometimes the groups of children flying to Britain brought little parcels for him from Lilya, containing chocolates and storybooks, and then Igor couldn't help but tell Barbara about Lilya and her cuddles and the way she softly sang to him at night. "Lilya is my granny," he explained. "She has grey hair and soft skin." Lilya wanted Igor to write to her. But he felt torn between his love for her and his fear that writing would somehow spoil everything and mean he'd have to go back. So Barbara wrote instead. Airports also presented a problem. Igor wanted to believe his Foster Mother wouldn't send him back, but how could he be certain? He was fearful of going to Heathrow airport to meet visiting children. Sometimes he would just march sulkily upstairs, take off his clothes and get into bed when Barbara announced they were going to the airport. But gradually, she was able to build up his confidence. Then in April, Barbara and Roy began discussing their annual two-week holiday to their time-share in Spain. Igor was invited, but he felt hesitant. Barbara had told him he would have to travel on an aeroplane, and this symbolized only one thing to him – the flight from uncomfortable memories. Eventually, though, he put his trust in Barbara and clambered up the steps of the plane by himself for the two-week holiday by the sea, whispering 'Spain' under his breath.

In July, Igor's bionic right arm was ready for the final fitting. Its length had been calculated so that it would be suitable for wear both with and without the boots. Alan slid the arm onto Igor's shoulder. There were straps that tucked around his other shoulder to make the arm secure, and Velcro buckles to fasten it tight. The arm was heavy – it weighed 1.35 kilos – but Igor was determined to master the intricate muscle movements that Alan showed him. Moving his shoulder blade would supply a charge that would exert a pull on a cable, and this would make the fingers of the electronic hand close tightly. Relaxing his shoulder would make the fingers open. He was told that eventually the movements would become second nature. Igor played exploratory games with the new arm. He slid his own fingers into the open palm of the plastic hand and made the fingers shut, quickly pulling his own hand away. Then he positioned his new hand over a sheet of paper, closed the fingers and picked it up. He then hopped up on his black boots, walked to the other end of the room, sat down and slid a pen between the new fingers. Holding it tight, he pulled off its lid with his left hand. He tried to write, but his new hand was at the wrong angle. To rotate its position, Igor had to grasp the new wrist and twist it around. He was then able to make his first tentative marks on paper with his new right hand. He then switched the biro to his left hand and quickly sketched two pictures of himself. One showed him on the way to hospital with only one arm, the other showed him with two arms.

Igor's new elbow wasn't electronically controlled. If he wanted it to bend, he had to move the lower arm to the angle he required. Pressing a button would fix it in position. If Igor found it easy to cope with the existing functions of the new arm, the team explained that they would be able to provide additional functions for him. If he wanted an electronically powered wrist or elbow, for example, they would be able to add one. Such an arm would cost over £4000. It was a very generous offer. After two hours experimentation, Igor had a request. "Can I

going to hospital

going home

Igor going to hospital with one arm, and going home with two

take it home," he said, "I want to cut my sausages." Before he let Igor leave with his new arm, Alan Stephenson turned his attention to the swiftly growing toe. This was also the perfect opportunity to refine the height of the heels. Although Igor liked the thirteen centimetre heels, he found they restricted his movement. Alan decided to produce a new pair of larger shoes, with eight centimetre tall heels, enabling him to move faster. Igor matter-of-factly asked Alan to get out his scissors and cut off his offending toe while he was at it.

Three months after Igor's arrival in Britain, Barbara and Victor began to think about his schooling. He had had some English lessons from a home tutor supplied by the local education authority and was able to hold proper conversations and to enjoy *Peter Pan*, his favourite story, which Barbara would read to him over and over at night. But she knew that if Igor were to stay in Britain, the authorities would expect him to be in full-time education. Teaching him at home wasn't an option because Barbara had no training. Only a school could do the job properly. She and Victor considered the possibilities for a while, but when it was clear Igor was going to stay in Britain beyond the six-month limit of his first visa, his education became a priority.

Igor was seven years old but had never spent a single hour at school. Not only that, but he had no idea what school was like – or even what it meant. He had been raised in a ward where every daily activity, apart from walking in the garden with Lilya, had taken place in the same confined space. Although he was used to having a daily routine broken into organised chunks for eating, sleeping and playing, the other children who shared this rota with him had been virtually silent. Igor had never heard the noisy excitement of a classroom or playground. His only conversations had been with Tamara, Lilya and the other nurses when they had the time. Structured schooling was vital. Precious time in Igor's development was ticking past. Ten minutes from Farncombe was the small village of Badshot Lea, and on the crossroads in the centre of the village 110 children, aged from four to seven, were divided into four classes in a pretty Victorian brick building called Badshot Lea County Infant School. Although it was a mainstream school, it had a Special Needs Unit attached for physically handicapped children. Around twenty of the pupils needed support for difficulties including visual impairment and cerebral palsy. The children in the unit were in mainstream classes for some subjects, and could receive extra support when required.

Barbara was initially hesitant. She wasn't certain that Igor should be segregated and made to feel different. He was clearly a quick learner. One day he had followed Roy outside and watched as he replaced the brake pads on the front left wheel of his car. When Roy began on the right-hand wheel, Igor passed him each tool as it was required. Eventually Barbara changed her mind when she realised that the presence of the special unit meant that other children in the school would be accustomed to seeing children with various disabilities. If Igor attended this school, it seemed unlikely he would be stared at or picked on, and if things did get too much for him, there was always the reassuring sanctuary of the unit to retreat to.

During the summer term of 1994, while Igor's future was being planned, Victor Mizzi drove to the primary school and took an assembly. The children sat cross-legged in their uniform of red sweatshirts and grey skirts and shorts. They listened as Victor showed pictures of the youngsters from Igor's children's home, including a large photograph of Igor. Victor explained that there had been a terrible accident in the former Soviet Union and hundreds of children were living in state orphanages. "They don't have the things you take for granted," said Victor. "You can brush your teeth in the mornings, but they haven't got any toothpaste. Your Mummy picks you up if you fall over, but they don't have mummies or daddies to cuddle them when they cry." He also told them that a boy called Igor had recently arrived in Britain to receive a bionic arm. The children asked a lot of perceptive questions. One boy wanted to know if the arm would rust if Igor went out in the rain. The children were keen to help the children they had heard about, so Victor asked them to donate useful gifts, such as toothpaste and soap, which he would take to the children's hospital in Minsk. Over the next week, several large cardboard boxes in the school secretary's office filled up with the items they brought in.

Near the end of term the headmistress, Mrs Norman, told the pupils that after the summer holidays they were going to have the little boy from Minsk joining them. She reminded them that Igor had short legs and only one arm. She knew it was important that when Igor first set foot in the playground, the other children didn't stare too hard or flock round him. The children had always been sensitive with pupils who looked slightly different, so she hoped her explanation would do the trick.

The Teacher

One Monday morning in September 1994 it was time for Igor's first day at school. The television production company had arrived early to film this momentous day in his life. Barbara pulled back the curtains in his bedroom and leaned over Igor, who was pretending to be asleep in his racing-car bed and trying to ignore the cameraman and soundman, tiptoeing around in his room with their whirring equipment. Barbara eventually coaxed Igor from under the covers by tickling his tummy. He went into the bathroom, pulled his blue plastic step up to the basin and cleaned his teeth, laughing at the film crew now crammed into the small space by the corner of the bath-tub. Igor dressed for school all by himself and Barbara fitted his bionic arm, carefully rolling up the right sleeve of his red school uniform sweatshirt with its white logo. Igor had been practising hard with his bionic arm all summer, but it wasn't quite what he had expected. No one had explained to him how heavy and hard it was going to be. But Alan Stephenson had reassured him that it was only the first prototype and that the technology would improve with further refinements.

In the kitchen, with just a few minutes to spare before the taxi arrived to take him and Barbara to the school, Igor asked for a pen and paper. By now he felt oblivious to the film crew; he had more important things to attend to. Barbara had taught him to write his own name and he painstakingly marked the four letters on a piece of cardboard. Then he called out, "Barba, how do you write love?"

"Igor, we haven't got time for all this," she replied. He felt crushed and repeated her name. She bustled over and quickly wrote the word in biro.

"Barba, how do you write Barba?" he inquired.

"Igor, you're going to be late." She added her name to the cardboard and shook herself as she suddenly realised what he had asked her to write. Yes, it was a token of security that he had wanted to leave at home during his first day at school as a permanent marker of his existence. But he had also dictated a declaration of deep attachment. Minutes later, sitting in the taxi with the cameraman and speeding to the school, Barbara asked him, "What are you going to say when the teacher asks your name?"

"Igor," he said in his deep voice.

"You have to say, 'My name is ...'" Barbara corrected him.

"My name is Igor," he boomed loudly, but he was feeling rather nervous when, five minutes later, Barbara led him through the gates of the gabled brick school. In fact, there were now hundreds of butterflies flapping madly on top of his breakfast. He clung to Barbara's hand, his heavy plastic arm weighing down his other shoulder. All the other children had gone inside. He looked back. The film crew were waving goodbye to him from the gate as they finished filming. Barbara led him in through the double doors, along the passages and into a bright room with a vast sand tray and lots of pictures on the walls. This looked like an exciting place to be. As he said goodbye to Barbara most of the butterflies had fluttered away. Soon he was absorbed in making sandcastles.

The teachers had decided that Igor should go into the reception class with the four- and five-year-olds. Certainly, they were a similar height to their new classmate and, like them, Igor had arrived without basic number or letter skills. The aim was to teach him the vital nuts and bolts of spelling, counting and writing. A less formal classroom, one with play equipment, sand and water, would also be a gentler introduction to school, rather than the challenge of joining children of his own age who already confidently knew the ropes. Igor knew enough rudimentary English to make his needs clear and to understand his teacher, Mrs Newport, and her simple instructions. Within a few days he was feeling tremendously confident as the taxi pulled up outside number 27. He would rush outside with his school rucksack slung over his left shoulder, yelling, 'Bye, Barba,' as he disappeared for more drawing, playing and learning. There was so much to do compared with the children's hospital in Minsk, where every day had seemed the same. He wanted to join in and try anything.

For the first few days the children did stare at Igor. They had never seen a child with legs like his and some of them thought they should offer to carry his bags, but Igor didn't like them looking at him. He wanted to play football or chase with the boys. So he did. There was a discreetly enforced rule that boys and girls were discouraged from taking their toys to school, but Igor loved bringing things in to show the other children. Usually he would bring in one of his ever-expanding collection of small model cars and fire engines. He delighted in confidently explaining all their special features. He would patiently show his class mates the miniature steering wheels that made the tyres change direction, and he would demonstrate how the doors and bonnets could open on tiny hinges. When Mrs Newport saw Igor chattering away in English about his fleet of shiny vehicles, she decided to encourage his enthusiasm and turned a blind eye to this bending of the rules. He had found his own natural way to learn the English language comfortably and confidently. Igor had speech therapy lessons once a week to develop his vocabulary, but the best way for children to learn a new language is to be immersed in an environment where they constantly hear it. His teachers tried to make Igor's lessons as visual as possible so he would understand what they were talking about. They would also give him a few minutes of extra supervision when everyone was settling down to a piece of work to ensure he knew what to do. Within a few months, Igor was conversing with relative ease. He was also getting the hang of the school week. One Monday morning he said to Barbara, "Today's Monday so I've got five days at school. But at the end of today, I'll only have four." He had also learned to dislike school lunches.

Near the beginning of term, the reception-class children were asked to draw or paint a picture of themselves. Igor sat down with a box of crayons and drew a smiling face. He then added one arm and short legs. His teacher was delighted to see a physically handicapped child who was so comfortable with who his self-image. The sketch radiated this happiness. In the nine months Igor spent at Badshot Lea, he never once complained about his disabilities. He did enjoy provoking a response in other people, however, perhaps as an antidote to the time spent in Minsk with children who were unable to interact with his games. He would wave and shout hello to Mrs Newport, and he enjoyed the praise he often received for his physical agility. Before too long, his natural exuberance began to distract the younger children in the reception class. At only four and five years of age, they quickly became overwhelmed by the natural clown three years their senior. The teachers decided it was time Igor was put among children of his own age. They felt confident that he now had the skills to cope, so after autumn half term Igor moved into Mrs Reid's class of seven-year olds.

Mrs Reid had first seen Igor when he had visited the school at the end of the summer term and had been struck by his smiling face and exuberant manner. She was on playground duty when he had executed his remarkable set of one-armed cartwheels across the tarmac during break on his first day. A well-built woman with short fair hair and blue eyes, she wore sparkling dangly earrings and colourful skirts. She and Igor admired each other immediately. He liked her cheerfulness and patience. She was impressed by the way he managed so well despite his physical limitations. He seemed able to adapt his little body to any task in an utterly unselfconscious manner and refused to say, 'I can't'. Even though he had jumped two classes, Igor continued to have his academic work supervised by the Special Needs Coordinator, Miss Falconer. She kept a careful eye on his progress. He studied art and science with his mainstream class and went to the unit for maths and English, so he was being given all the help he needed. One day, Mrs Reid decided to teach her seven year olds about tessellations – shapes which could interlink and be repeated over and over again without spaces or any overlapping. It was a complex concept to grasp and Mrs Reid had always had varying success with her young pupils. Igor drew the shape he wanted to use. It was an unusual and elegant design, and Mrs Reid was surprised by its complexity. She wondered how he would handle cutting it out and linking it together with its repeat. She watched as he slid the paper to the edge of the table, wedged it under his wrist, picked up the scissors and used his chin to hold the paper still while he cut out the shape over and over again. He had soon accumulated a pile of the delicate paper pieces. Elsewhere, false starts were screwed up and plopped off desks onto the floor, but Igor was entirely absorbed. He coloured in each repeat carefully, before picking up the glue and sticking his shapes down next to one another on a clean sheet of paper. He produced a perfect, neat, tessellated pattern with no gaps or wobbly parts. It was the best example the class produced that day.

From then on, Mrs Reid never had to think to herself, "How is Igor going to cope with this?" He tackled physical education lessons with the same confidence, swinging from metal rings, clinging to ropes, somersaulting and cartwheeling. He was one of the most agile children in the class. During hockey lessons the children were issued with lightweight, full-length hockey sticks and told to tap the balls across the playing field, hitting them gently enough to keep then under control. Igor was dwarfed by his hockey stick, but he seized it with his single hand, and sped across the field, the dribbled ball running neatly in front of him. When he was changing for PE, he would take off his socks and scamper around in his bare feet. Because he was not self-conscious about his unusual feet and missing toes, the other children felt comfortable too.

The school had an outdoor swimming pool for use in the summer, but every week throughout the year the special needs unit would make a weekly trip by minibus to the Olympic-sized indoor pool at Aldershot. Igor had been nervous of water when he first arrived in Britain, but after his Spanish holiday by the pool, he now adored swimming. Although the children's pool at Aldershot was too deep for him to stand up in, he would launch himself at a float and drift off, using his feet like fins. Within a few months, he had dispensed with the float and designed his own one-armed splashy front crawl. It was a good thing he always wore goggles and held his breath. He also spent a lot of time propelling his streamlined body along underwater with his muscled arm, gazing at the shiny blue tiles. He liked to see everyone's legs jumping up and down in slow motion and churning up bubbles. He relished the aquatic environment where he was able to slice effortlessly through the water, like an otter. In the changing room one day, a four-year-old boy was transfixed by the sight of Igor's missing limbs.

"Where is your arm?" he asked innocently. "Oh, I knocked if off this morning when I was getting dressed," said Igor without hesitating.

He was supposed to wear his bionic arm at school, but he struggled with the cumbersome pink plastic. The arm was awkward and heavy. It felt too bulky to keep strapped on to his shoulder all day long, so he often hid it in his school bag. His teachers encouraged him to learn to use it to eat with a knife and fork, but it was always a battle. The only time Igor looked unhappy at school was when he was trying to cope with balancing a fork in that weighty hand and arm. He was also supposed to wear it during PE lessons to help his balance, but he found it actually impaired his ability to run, bounce and leap safely. When the teachers saw he was struggling with it, they relented. They would let him take it off at playtime and Igor, in his crafty manner, would 'forget' to put it back on again afterwards. But he wasn't too worried. A better, lighter arm was being developed for him that would function as a paperweight and hold his exercise books still.

Igor's understanding of English continued to improve. He loved story-telling time and would sit absolutely still, concentrating hard on the narration without fidgeting. Mrs Reid could tell that Igor really understood the gist of the story because he would eagerly discuss it, and even ask the meanings of unfamiliar words. He picked up joined-up writing swiftly, helped by a sheet of flat blue plastic lent by the Special Needs Unit. It anchored his paper to the desk and stopped it sliding around. He was also given his own low chair and table in the classroom. It was intended for his safety, but Igor hated being closer to the ground than the other children. He knew he was just as capable of flopping his tummy onto an ordinary chair and pulling himself upright with his powerful left arm, spinning his short legs up on to the seat. As the academic year wore on, he would drag a spare full-size chair over to a full-size desk and sit with the other children. In art classes he would stand up on the plastic seat and so would be as tall as the other children who were standing up and daubing paint onto paper.

The children related to Igor as they would to any other child. He always found making friends easy because of his confident approach to other people. He was a very social child and was swiftly absorbed into groups at school and at home. He also saw no difference between him and other children and felt no resentment at other children's bodies. Because he behaved like an equal, other children treated him as one. In Minsk Igor had grown up without the concept of a 'best friend' so his approach was much more straightforward. If someone was fun Igor would get great enjoyment from them. Neither was he possessive of the children he played with, so he quickly had a wide circle of friends. Barbara noticed that he had a trusting attitude to other people, whatever their age. Every week he spoke of different adventures with a mix of new names. His early experiences had given him an independent and self-contained personality. Watching him, Barbara was once again overwhelmed by his apparent lack of emotional problems, despite his challenging start to life.

Igor was still absorbed by fire engines and firemen. He loved to draw and to paint, so his artistic ability was usually poured into intricate pictures of fire-fighting scenes. They were filled with all the colourful details that create a sense of drama: flames leaping into the sky, cascades of water dousing them down and billowing black smoke. Firemen in helmets would climb up the ladders to rescue people trapped on the top floor of houses, or douse the ferocious orange- and red-flecked flames with bright blue water jets. He loved to use a rainbow of different colours. All his artwork was neatly done.

One day Igor worked with a partner to make a model tree house to illustrate a story called A *Tree House for Monster*. He relished cutting up and glueing shoe boxes together, and designing paper furniture to go inside. He also found sewing surprisingly easy. He was able to press the fabric against the table with his body, while using his hand to control needle and thread. He was proud of the mouse finger-puppet he made from felt. He also contributed towards a class embroidery frieze of the village. Igor also liked working the school computers and found it very easy to coordinate the different functions on the keyboard and use the mouse. Barbara encouraged his interest, hoping it could lead to a more realistic choice of career in the future. When it came to writing stories, Igor was not yet at a stage where he was able to spell and write down a whole sequence of thoughts, so Mrs Reid would ask him to tell her the story behind one of his drawings. Sometimes she asked him to draw a sequence of pictures to tell a story. Of course, these usually featured police cars, fire engines and houses in flames.

The Foster Family

As Christmas 1994 approached, Igor had settled very well in year two at school. He was keeping his clowning down to manageable levels and if anyone asked why he didn't have an arm he would simply reply, 'I didn't get one'. There were times when he was in trouble for being over-exuberant or disobeying teachers, but no more than any other child. Mrs Reid was delighted with his progress. He was familiar with numbers from one to twenty and was quickly absorbing the vocabulary of mathematical terms: larger, shorter, lighter, and so on. Sometimes he needed reassurance after she had set him off on a piece of work. He would stop and quietly bring it to her for her encouragement. Then he would happily return to his desk and continue. By the end of the winter term, he was able to read the early stages of the stage two green books in the *Oxford Reading Tree* and felt a great sense of achievement when he read an entire book independently. During music lessons Igor was happy to express himself. He had a good sense of rhythm and would join in the singing with enthusiasm. He also liked playing accompaniments on the tambourine and triangle.

Igor had spent three months surrounded by children from loving homes. It was inevitable that he should begin to crave the intimacy of a family of his own. One day during the Christmas holidays, when the Bennetts' house was filled with brightly coloured tinsel and a statuesque Christmas tree which he and Barbara had festooned with glittering decorations, and Igor was sitting at the kitchen table surrounded by paper and felt-tips, he suddenly said to Barbara, "I've made you a drawing." His picture showed a neatly drawn, carefully coloured-in fire engine. Above it, he had written, 'to Mummy and Daddy'. In the children's home Igor had had no concept of families, so this was the first time he had referred to her and Roy in this way. Initially Barbara was surprised he could write the words and she was moved by the inference of the words. Igor had become extremely attached to her and Roy. Barbara felt hugely emotional about his expression of affection, but her pleasure was mixed with consternation. She didn't know what the future held for Igor. She was worried by the strength of his attachment to her and Roy. Could she allow herself to return his love, secure in the sense that it could be ongoing?

She was aware that it was school that had encouraged him to begin craving family. It had also created in him a desire for information about human relationships. For some time he had wanted to know why some people called

Barbara and Roy 'Granny' and 'Grandad'. And when their daughter Debbie was pregnant, he'd asked Barbara hopefully, but without too much conviction, "Did I grow in your tummy?" Barbara had pinched him and said, "Don't be silly, you've only been in England for a little while". Igor then tried another tack, "I wasn't born a baby, I was born a boy, ready to come to England."

More pictures of his "Mummy" followed, usually with bright green hair, a fashion detail that he quickly discovered was guaranteed to send her swooping upon him noisily. When Barbara's grandson Toby was born, Igor's first question was, "Does he have both arms and legs?" Barbara had recently told Igor in vague terms about his past. "There was a nasty bang at a factory making electricity. Your real Mummy lived nearby and a thing called radiation made her ill. That's why you haven't grown properly." Igor continued to speak only fleetingly of Belarus, and in mainly negative terms. Sometimes he would say, "We have that in Minsk, but not as good". He was still reluctant to speak Russian, but Barbara was aware he needed to be reminded of his culture and was worried that he would forget his native language. Roy had a Russian-speaking friend who came to visit them sometimes, but Igor would stride across the patio-garden shutting out the all too familiar words. "I'm English, I don't need to speak Russian," he once spat.

Victor Mizzi realised it would be in Igor's best interests to stay in Britain for a longer period so that he could continue to be helped by Steeper's who had offered to treat him for free. He made an application to the immigration department for another extension to his visa. In March 1995, Igor met his local MP, Virginia Bottomley, then Secretary of State for Health, at the local government offices in Godalming. He embraced the politician with his strong right arm and she promised to do all she could to help his cause. After this meeting she wrote to Victor:

I would like to say how moved I was to meet Igor last week. The world is full of people who identify problems. Those who decide to take practical steps to improve the circumstances of fellow human beings deserve the highest praise. I would like to send my warmest congratulations to you and all those involved in his care, to whom I hope you will pass on my best wishes: Mr Tucker, Mr Stephenson and of course, Barbara.

One day Barbara told Igor that soon it would be his eighth birthday. Igor was confused, "But, Mummy, I've already had a birthday." Barbara explained that birthdays and birthday parties are an annual event. Igor looked downcast. When she asked him why, he said he wasn't ready to return his toys just yet, so when she told them he could still keep them he was delighted. For his birthday treat, Barbara said that he could choose four or five friends to take to Bird World near Aldershot. Igor was very popular and most of his friends were active, tough little boys who loved to kick a football. But among his birthday guests was Sophia, one of the kindest girls in his class. Igor's best friend was seven-year-old Lee, a quiet, sensitive boy who didn't push himself forward and was very thoughtful.

Igor went to another special birthday party in March. The Duchess of York invited him and a group of visiting Belarussian children suffering from cancer to Princess Eugenie's fifth party. It was held at the Royal Berkshire Hotel in Sunninghill, outside Ascot, close to her home on the Wentworth Estate. Large rugs were spread on the smooth lawns and Igor sat as guest of honour with Fergie and her daughters, the Princesses Beatrice and Eugenie. They were entranced by the witty little boy, as they played with balloons together. There was a massive cake with five candles, a juggler and a clown. When the clown asked for a volunteer for a trick, Igor's arm shot into the air. The Duchess saw her daughters' delight with Igor. From then on, if they complained or were badly behaved, she would remind them about Igor and how he didn't make a fuss, despite his disability.

Victor continued to receive letters and money from people who were reading articles and watching television items about Igor's progress. Victor always replied to each letter, regardless of whether any money was enclosed inside the envelopes. Many letters were from children who found it easy to identify with Igor's lively manner. He kept them all.

On notepaper with colourful elephants striding across it, a girl named Charley wrote to Victor in large black handwriting:

Dear Mr Mizzi,
    I have saved up my pocket money and now I have got six pounds.

Please could you send the money to the children in Russia. Or buy some medicines and then send it to Russia. Thank you Mr Mizzi.

Love from Charley xxx

During the holidays, two girls called Katy McEvoy and Emma Perkins held a fete in Katy's parents' garden in Surrey to which Igor was invited. They raised £150 for the charity:

Dear Mr Mizzi,

We had a lovely time yesterday. We were really glad that Igor could come and he had a great time. At the end Igor wanted us to throw wet sponges at him, so we threw gently and he said to throw them harder. But even that wasn't enough for him so he filled a bucket of water and poured it over his head. He also did somersaults and cartwheels all over the garden. He won on mini golf and made a determined effort on the pinball. We made sure he went home with lots of prizes. We hope that this enclosed cheque will help bring over another child from Russia.

Yours sincerely,

Katy and Emma.

PS. I might have another fete next year.

Igor joined his foster parents for his second Spanish holiday in May 1995. He practised his swimming strokes under the baking sun and turned a healthy brown. He giggled as he asked the barman for Roy's vodka, but when he returned to school he had an alarming tale to tell his class. He recalled how he and the Bennetts had been involved in a dramatic air-sea rescue. They had gone on a boat trip around the bay, but got into difficulties with the heavy sea. A helicopter had picked them up from their sinking dinghy, but as the rescue noose was slipped around Igor's waist it had slipped off because of his single arm and he had nearly plunged into the waves. Igor's teacher, Mrs Reid, anxiously phoned Barbara to see if she was recovering well after her ordeal. Barbara didn't know what she was talking about. The whole story was a product of Igor's fertile imagination – he loved playing practical jokes. When Mrs Reid confronted him, he laughed heartily at his power to persuade adults in his new language. She was secretly impressed with his eye for detail.

At the end of March, after Igor had been in Britain for 14 months, a Social Worker visited the Bennetts to review his progress. She typed up a two-page report with her observations:

Igor is used to the comings and goings of a busy household and enjoys social contact. Emotionally he seems to have formed a close bond with Roy and Barbara, and since Christmas has referred to them as his Mummy and Daddy. I understand he became quite angry when others did not follow his lead. At the same time, Barbara has begun to explore with him the question of his real parents and he understands that she is not his natural mother, nor Roy his natural father. Barbara is taking her lead from Igor in this. She is moving at his pace and giving him information as he demands it.

Generally on my visits Igor seems a happy child, who is comfortable with his environment and himself. Barbara and Roy, however, are aware that as he grows older, Igor may have to face emotional and psychological problems in adjusting to his disabilities. They are prepared to seek whatever help he may need.

Igor seems like a normal eight year old boy who likes to get his own way. He can be tenacious in pursuing his own ends. There is a danger that other children may sometimes over-compensate for him, but he is encouraged by Barbara and Roy to be self-reliant.

Igor is not allowed to forget his Russian heritage. Although reluctant to speak Russian, it is apparent that he does understand the language. Barbara hopes that at some point it may be possible to visit Minsk with him. She uses every opportunity to discuss with him his cultural background. This foster placement continues to provide Igor with a loving and supportive foster home. Igor views the Bennett's home as his home and it gives him a secure and stable base.

Victor was pleased to read the Social Worker's positive conclusions about Igor's new life with Barbara and Roy, but the fact that nothing was known of the boy's birth parents in Belarus was on his mind. Had they died, or was there another reason why he was signed over to the authorities after his birth? These were questions that were to cause Victor increasing consternation over the coming years. He could see that his involvement in Igor's life was to be a long-standing arrangement, and he knew that he owed to it him to try and find answers to difficult questions about his heritage.

Igor still was untroubled by such matters. His world consisted of daily life with his foster parents and his dream of becoming a fireman when he grew up. The red toy fire engine that Vic Tucker had given him had been his first real hint of the outside world and its influence continued to hold firm. Barbara encouraged his passion and brought him a yellow plastic fireman's hat. He would scale the climbing frame in the garden, pretending he was at the top of an extending ladder, and the magnificent sound of a real fire engine tearing along the road had him racing to the garden fence. When *Daily Express* photographer Larry Ellis came to take photographs one summer afternoon, Igor refused to cooperate until we agreed to watch him douse imaginary flames roaring out of his wooden Wendy house in the garden and rescue an imaginary damsel. It didn't matter how many times Barbara gently hinted at the practical problems concerning his chosen career, Igor would not be swayed from his ambition. If she said, "You've only got one arm", he would say, "I'm going to hold the hose". If she hinted at his little legs, he would simply say, "I won't drive, I'll be one of the ones in the back".

One of the most exciting days of Igor's life was when he met the cast of his favourite television series, *London's Burning*, in June 1995. Within minutes of meeting his heroes, he had taken over the London Weekend Television film set. Igor had become hooked on the long-running series as soon as he saw it, even before he understood the words. When he watched a story that spanned two episodes he said, "The firemen must be so tired – they've been fighting the fire all week while I've been at school." One summer afternoon, Victor and Barbara took him to Shropshire for a party with some other Chernobyl children. The local fire brigade brought their engine along to show them. It was Igor's third ride in a fire engine; he had already been to the stations in Godalming and Guildford. On each occasion he would sit in the front seat making appropriate sound effects and feeling wonderfully proud.

Igor was now the oldest boy at Badshot Lea County Infant School and at the end of the summer term, in July 1995, it was time for him to leave. If he had been blessed with a complete body, the teachers agreed he would have been as tall as the tallest boys at the school. Igor had worked so hard that his year spent in the small village school had really paid off. At the beginning, Barbara had simply hoped that he would enjoy himself and hadn't hoped for more than a zero in his National Curriculum Assessment grades. Instead he passed Key Stage One with grade 1 in every subject: reading, writing and maths. This was the same grade as children who had been at the school for three years, not just nine months. Mrs Reid's end of year report glowed with praise:

Igor is a confident, well-adjusted child who enjoys life to the full. He makes friends easily and is friendly with adults and children alike. He is bright, alert and learns quickly. He participates in every area of the curriculum, and has produced some lovely, careful pieces of work. He listens attentively and enjoys offering his own thoughts and ideas. He has persevered with the English language and is able to converse fluently. He loves books and particularly enjoys having stories read to him, and talking about the pictures. Igor is extremely agile in PE and shows no fear or apprehension at all. He compensates for his 'disability' remarkably well and joins in all activities with gusto. Igor has an enquiring mind and has settled into school life exceptionally well. He has done extremely well to achieve Level 1 in maths, reading and writing and I am sure he will continue to make progress when he moves on to the junior school.

Igor had found his first bionic arm heavy and somewhat difficult to control, so Steeper's designed him another one without the electronic hand. It was a cosmetic arm which served two purposes: he could roll down his sleeve over it to give the impression of two arms and it also made the perfect anchor for his school work. Resting the arm on the paper, he was able to hold his exercise books perfectly still and draw a straight line. It was like a liberation: the ultimate portable paperweight. During the summer holidays Igor's dream of playing soccer came true when Steeper's presented him with a surprise: his own special pair of custom-built football boots with coloured laces and proper black studs on the base. He hadn't been able to kick a ball on grass before, because his other shoes didn't grip. Laced into his new boots, he was soon tearing around in the garden at Queen Mary's Hospital. Igor hoped that he would be able to play real football at his new school. Victor and Barbara were still discussing exactly where his education was to continue.

One day during the holidays, some nine-year old boys knocked on Barbara's door to ask if Igor could come out to play. She reluctantly told them that he was too small and might get hurt. Twenty minutes later, as she weeded the front garden, she heard cheering and shouting down the road. She put down her secateurs and stood up, brushing grass from her knees. Igor was perched on a skateboard, whizzing down the centre of the road. The two older boys were running alongside him, ready to catch him if he fell. But he kept his gaze level and his arm outstretched for balance. His little body was flexing like a reed in the wind to help him to steady himself. The skateboard gradually rolled to a halt and Igor jumped off. During the holidays Igor often visited an adventure playground for special needs children near Guildford. Once he excitedly told Barbara about scrambling up the climbing frame and mentioned his 'friend'. Intrigued, Barbara stayed to watch after she had dropped him off one day. She saw Igor immediately run to the side of a young girl in an electric wheelchair. Igor guided her carefully through the playground, running along by her side. When she approached a slope or dip he would say, "Slower, slower". As the path levelled out he would check ahead and urge her on, "Alright, fast now." She responded by pressing the controls of her wheelchair to pick up speed. Barbara asked a playground worker who the girl was. 'Igor's girlfriend,' was the answer.

In September 1995, Igor started at the William Cobbett County Junior School in Farnham with 400 children aged eight to twelve. He was to be part of the Special Needs Unit there, but would take some lessons with his classmates, just as before. Igor missed his old teacher. After his first day at the new school, he said forlornly to Barbara, "Why didn't Mrs Reid come with me?" Igor's new eight-year old classmates were happy to play football with him. They were tolerant of his needs and indulged him by slipping the ball to him. But Igor wanted more. His ambition was to play with the big boys. One lunch time, he put his feet inside the new bespoke football boots and strode into their playground territory. He nearly collided with one of the twelve-year-olds, who was racing with the ball and didn't see the tiny boy who was gazing eagerly at the nifty footwork. He just avoided knocking Igor over like a skittle. The big boys shouted at Igor and told him to get out of the way. He felt utterly dejected as he wandered back to the younger boys, cursing his body and his short legs that made his dreams impossible. Sometimes even playing with friends was a frustration. If he went to give the ball a hard kick, he often fell over when his boots made contact with the ball. Barbara knew it was vital to stand back and let him discover his own limitations, but she didn't always find it easy when he came home miserable.

In October Igor was admitted to a London hospital for exploratory surgery. There was a danger that his body might harbour a cancerous growth that, although invisible now, might grow into a tumour in the future. It was a tense time. No one could predict whether the radiation that had led to his congenital deformities would have affected him in other ways. Victor had contacted Tamara, in Belarus, for her permission for the operation to take place. The surgeon could find no evidence of any cancerous growths. Twenty-four hours after his surgery, he was allowed home. Victor and his wife, Birgitta, came with Valentina, the Belarussian Charity coordinator, to see Igor at home. They expected to find him lying quietly in bed. To their surprise, he was in the sitting room playing with his toys. As soon as he saw them, he jumped on the sofa and pulled up his jumper to show off the little scar, with no inhibitions at all. For the next two weeks this was normal practice, until Barbara gently persuaded him that he had shown enough people.

In November, Barbara asked Igor if he would like to go back to Minsk for a holiday one day. He didn't answer and disappeared up to his room. His fears about being sent back seemed as strong as ever. Barbara and Victor both felt that a short trip in the future to visit Lilya and Tamara would be important for his emotional development, but only if he would definitely be able to return to England afterwards. Barbara had grown deeply attached to Igor and after 18 months she couldn't visualise life without him. "He's really my little boy in lots and lots of ways," she told the documentary film makers with tears welling up in her eyes. "Every morning I tell myself, 'He's not yours, he's borrowed, you can't love him,' but all the logical things go out of the window … There are some children you can just feed and clothe, but not Igor." She was dazzled by his positive attitude to life, despite his inauspicious beginnings in an institution, and by his self-possessed enthusiasm. After nearly two years she felt as if he had been part of her family forever. She adored his imagination, his impish sense of humour, his eye for detail and his lively confidence. But she had begun to fear that someone might try to take him away from her. So on 9 December 1995, Victor Mizzi approached the High Court in London about this issue. The Judge's verdict was positive. Igor was to reside with Barbara Bennett for as long as his visa allowed him to remain in Britain. No one could remove him without the approval of the Wardship Court.

But Victor was still uncertain for how long Igor would be allowed to stay in Britain. As time went on, documents about Igor were being shuffled between various government departments. Their local MP and old ally, Virginia Bottomley, who had been so moved by Igor when they met, had also been working on his behalf, firing off letters to Home Secretary Michael Howard. But the expiry date on Igor's visa was fast approaching. Victor spent hours welded to his phone, cajoling and pleading with countless civil servants on Igor's behalf. On 9 February 1996, just two weeks before Igor's residency visa was due to expire, Victor's perseverance paid off. A letter from Virginia Bottomley dropped through the letter box:

I am pleased to send you a copy of the letter I received this morning from the Home Secretary, the Rt Hon Michael Howard QC MP. Igor Pavlovets has been granted leave to remain for a further two years until 25th February 1998. This is good news indeed. Please pass on my best wishes to Igor. Do let us keep in close touch.

Attached was a letter signed by Michael Howard that said:

At the end of this period Mr Mizzi may re-apply on Igor's behalf for further leave to remain when again his application will be given sympathetic consideration.

Victor was overjoyed and deeply grateful for British justice and compassion, but still his nagging concerns about the identity of Igor's real parents continued.

The Dead Zone

In 1994, shortly after Igor started school in Surrey, I was invited to visit Belarus by Victor Mizzi and Chernobyl Children Life Line to report on the country for the *Daily Express*. We travelled south to the town of Bragin, the largely abandoned rural town that lies near the barbed wire entry to the enforced evacuation zone. Many of Bragin's small wooden houses have been looted and abandoned. The population of 17,000 has shrivelled to a quarter of that size after people realised that they were living on contaminated land, despite the contradictory information that was circulating after the disaster.

We set off towards the dead zone in a cream-coloured Lada. Purple nylon curtains swung in the back window and a small red plastic skeleton dangled ominously from the rear-view mirror. We slipped into the flat plains of the countryside and drove through forests along a deserted, ramrod straight road that stretched into the distance. We negotiated potholes the size of bathtubs. As we drew nearer, people were toiling in small fields, digging and hoeing the deceptively perfect looking soil, but soon these scarecrow-like figures dwindled. A solitary figure on a bicycle peddled past … a horse pulled a cart.

We pushed on, deeper into the desolate countryside. Our driver dictated a list of chilling instructions as we approached the 'dead zone', just thirty kilometres from the doomed reactor and our translator interpreted: Do not touch anything. Do not put your hands to your mouth. Do not breathe deeply and, above all, try to stay on the tarmac.

We saw the official checkpoint ahead and tension filled the car. We had no permit to enter the area because it is difficult to get official approval, but as we approached the wooden hut, a bored-looking soldier in a heavy greatcoat, waved us through. Teenagers on National Service are often posted to man these bleak outposts. As we accelerated past him, we saw ominous signs nailed to wooden stakes. A bright yellow symbol with three small, but menacing, arrows pointing to its centre carried the words: 'Radiation Danger: It is prohibited to grow and collect agricultural products, to make hay and to raise cattle.' A white sign painted with jagged black letters was stuck into the ground near woodland, it read: 'Danger of radiation. Entry and exit prohibited.' The road we were travelling along had been resurfaced in an effort to limit the radiation. For two hours, if you are careful, you are safe. The land either side of us was radioactively hot, yet it looked so tranquil. It was easy to imagine why the disorientated former inhabitants had found it impossible to believe that their fertile land had been made unworkable by an invisible contaminant. All you can do is look for symbols of decay, like the hay in the fields that has not been cut for ten years that now looks like long, untidy hair, laying rotting on the unturned soil. There are pylons but no power, slack phone-lines with no connections. And all the time your body is clocking up an unseen radiation dose that you cannot control. The sense of claustrophobia is intense.

The village of Bartolomeevka, 400 kilometres from Minsk, is like a cemetery. It was abandoned in 1989, when the villagers were forced to leave all their irradiated possessions behind. A narrow road stretches through the centre of this typical abandoned village. Outside one house is a rusting pushchair with a rotten fabric seat. On the overgrown grass in front of another, a hand-turned wooden cot painted bright green rests at a jaunty angle. Some of the struts are broken and the paint is peeling away. The picket fences that would once have marked out neat gardens, now choked with weeds, have also rotted. I broke the rules for a moment and picked and poked my way into one of the pretty houses, originally painted in bright boiled-sweet shades, that are disintegrating into the ground. The front door had rocked off its rusty hinges, and the tendrils of botanic invaders had snaked their way in through the broken glass of the hand-carved window-frames. The floorboards had collapsed into the cellar, and floral wallpaper was growing new, unexpected mould patterns. In the kitchen there were chipped china cups, bottles and cooking pots, all standing as they had been left. In the front room lay a pair of small red patent leather shoes, and near the fire grate was an unloved doll with dirty blonde hair and broken legs, reclining in the dust and rat droppings. On the wall above her hung a black-and-white photograph of a little girl with a bow in her hair. The glass was smashed, but the child stared out defiantly through the shards.

As I ran back onto the tarmac a hunched woman scuttled from the shadows. The woman, in her sixties, looked like a scarecrow in her tattered brown rags. She told us that she hadn't been able to comprehend the idea of leaving the only home she had ever known, so she and her brothers had refused to go and now she was tending the graves she had dug for them when they died. She invited us into her disintegrating, irradiated house though a dilapidated gate. She had a clay oven where she cooks the turnips and potatoes that she grows. In the corner lurked a skinny cat with a backbone like a coat hanger. All the while our driver remained alert. The police check car could come at any moment – you face arrest if you have entered and stopped without a permit. He glanced at his watch and signalled us back to the car. Soon we had left the sombre village, driving on past an abandoned school where all the glass in the windows had been smashed to the ground. Ten kilometres further on, two more rag-shrouded elderly people stood in a concrete bus shelter, waiting for a bus that will never arrive. There are barbed-wire fences near the road, behind which the land had been excavated and fall-out from the reactor buried in shallow graves. Skeletal cranes stand abandoned, rearing their rusty necks towards the grey sky above. Just a little while longer you dare yourself as you sneak into another house and off the tarmac. One more photograph can't make any difference, can it? We drove to within four kilometres of the border with Ukraine before beginning our escape in drizzle. The rain was lucky for us – the area is more dangerous when it is hot and dusty, with a wind that can whip contaminated particles into your face. Plants were growing between cracks in the tarmac. Not everything here is dead.

The villagers from farming communities like Bartolomeevka have been moved to the high-rise blocks in Minsk. Immediately following the disaster, 24,700 people were bussed out after the radioactive dust had fallen on their homes in areas registering fifteen or more curies of radiation per square kilometre. To date, more than 100,000 people have been permanently relocated from their homes in areas of ten to fifteen curies. Anyone living in an area with up to ten curies was doomed to stay, despite the health risks. Later, during our week-long visit, we visited the Minsk micro-districts where countless nine-story blocks contain broken elevators, forcing the inhabitants to trudge up and down the tiled stairs. Outside, there is no grass and nearby shops sell only basic foodstuffs such as eggs and bread and pickled onions. Fresh produce is hard to come by. It is difficult for people from the country to adapt to life in a small apartment, without land to tend.

In one of the blocks we met thirty-one-year-old Vera Afanasianco, one of the last villagers to be resettled with her children, seven-year-old Dimar and ten-year-old Anton. She has few possessions: two dining room chairs, a sofa bed, a cracked vase, cooking equipment, clothing and sheets, and an antiquated television with a flickering picture. When her family was relocated from the contaminated area, they were forced to leave everything behind. There are no pictures on the walls and a stale smell fills her two-room flat, which is wall-to-wall linoleum. "I am terrified my children will develop cancer," she says looking out across the concrete. "We had to wait five years in the contaminated area until we reached the top of the housing list. There is not a single day we don't long for our chickens and our home."

If Igor was at school in Minsk, his education couldn't be more different to the cosy and constructive environment of his school in Surrey. Vera's children, like the other refugees in the drab high-rises, attend schools in the micro-districts. With over 2000 pupils, many of these schools are like education factories. Because of the high demand for lessons and a shortage of money to build new schools, each day exhausted teachers run two entirely separate school days, with two different sets of pupils. The first lessons start at seven a.m. until two p.m. The second sitting begins at two p.m. and finishes six hours later. Inside School Six, there are gloomy passages leading to cheerless classrooms. There is no grass nor playing fields beyond the pebble-dash walls, no trees or flowers, just a large patch of mud. Since 1991, Belarussian school children have been receiving environmental lessons that teach them about radiation. They learn about its characteristics and are instructed how to behave safely in contaminated areas. The deputy headmistress of School Six was surprisingly bubbly and jovial. She was also immensely dedicated. She is paid just £15 a month and out of this the photocopying costs for her pupils to learn English have to be drawn. The school has no photocopier of its own and she has just one English language textbook. Because she thinks it important that her students are given the opportunity to learn English, she had arranged to have some of the larger classrooms converted into several smaller language labs. The wallpaper is badly stuck to the damp walls and peeling at the edges. At least this school is not located in a contaminated area. Over 2,000 schools in Belarus are trying to operate in the hot zone. Many of them have no central heating, no running water, no sewage system, no sports hall and no canteen. Many of them are desperately short of teachers.

The health impacts of the Chernobyl accident are difficult to measure, but the Belarussian government estimated in 1995 that there were one million children disabled, damaged or diseased as a consequence of the disaster. Between 1990 and 1994, many types of health disorders among the children of Belarus increased. UNICEF figures for the mid-nineties showed that defects of the heart and circulatory system had gone up by 43 per cent, disorders of the nervous system by 43 per cent, disorders of the digestive organs by 28 per cent, disorders of the bone, muscle and connective tissues by 62 per cent, anaemia by 10 per cent and asthma by 48 per cent. Cancer of the thyroid is one of the most serious problems. Between 1966 and 1985 twenty-one children in Belarussia required surgery, but between 1986 and 1994 that figure swelled to 329 operations. "These figures will continue to climb every year for the next 400 years," predicts Dr Reiman Ismailzade, who runs a children's cancer hospital near Minsk. "I am seeing types of cancer that before I only read about in textbooks." Medicine is in desperately short supply. "Resources are so slim here that if we use a needle only a thousand times we consider we are being extravagant," he says. When Victor Mizzi hands

Dr Ismailzade a suitcase of drugs, the doctor immediately calls his staff. Within ten minutes the first children are being injected with the anti-nausea serums brought by the Charity.

Igor, despite his physical disability, is one of the lucky children of Chernobyl. He has been given a new life. A 1993 health survey examined 500 Belarussian children and found only one to be completely healthy. Yet the only official monument in Belarus to the ongoing tragedy is in a park in Minsk. Shaded by trees, three lumps of highly polished stone the size of coffins face the road. Every year, on 26 April, these jet-black stones are shrouded in drifts of blood red carnations and roses. Loudspeakers from a van blare rousing music and a clutch of people stand with lighted candles. Speeches are made, people cry, the music plays. A few hours later the memorial is once again deserted.

The Future

As the first edition of this book goes to press, Igor is just two weeks short of his ninth birthday on 29 March 1996. He speaks almost perfect English and his left arm grows more powerful by the day, although he no longer uses it like a third leg. He delights in arm-wrestling his visitors and, of course, he always wins. Unknown to him, he continues to draw attention to the plight of the other children of Chernobyl, left behind on contaminated land, and he has become a symbol of their plight.

Barbara's house is filled with Igor's favourite toys. But he still asks after his first red fire engine, which is with the other children at the children's hospital in Minsk. His new possessions include a plastic petrol-filling station. Igor is also an avid Lego model-builder and the lowest shelf in his bedroom is dedicated to his carefully constructed Lego scenes of fire stations. He still dreams of being a fireman and his drawings of engines grow ever more precise. The Carlton documentary about Igor's life, *Igor: Child of Chernobyl*, was shown on Tuesday 6 June 1995. Igor stayed up late to watch the hour-long programme, which included footage from children's hospitals in Minsk, including the one where he used to live. The only part he didn't enjoy was hearing himself singing an improvised carol on Christmas day. "I asked them not to put that bit in," he told Barbara, indignantly. The next morning he went to school as usual. Barbara's and Victor Mizzi's phones began ringing again with offers of help and money to help support Igor and other children affected by the Chernobyl disaster. The duty officer at Carlton confirmed that the response from the public was unprecedented. Haslemere Post Office was again swamped by 5,000 letters, many writers inquiring as to how they could help the children of Chernobyl shown in the film. The result was 150 tonnes of aid donated by pharmaceutical companies and schools that ran appeals for food and clothes. Viewers also organised fundraising activities nationwide, including sponsored walks, runs and rides, gala concerts, bring-and-buy sales and charity dinners. The documentary has since been shown in many other countries and won eight major television awards. A letter from the Embassy of the Republic of Belarus, in London, was among those received by the Charity. Officials there were deeply grateful for the publicity the film had given to the plight of their people: 'One of the main values of the film is that ordinary people have not been indifferent to the grief of our nation.'

Ask Igor if he will return to Minsk and he scratches his wavy brown hair, looks wistful and says, "Yes, but only for a holiday". He now feels more secure about returning to airports. Recently he and Barbara drove to Heathrow with Victor, who had forgotten to buckle his seat belt. In the terminal Igor saw two policemen patrolling with guns, so he ran up to them and told them that they should arrest Victor for not doing up his seat belt. On another visit to the airport he spotted a businessman with a mobile phone and asked if he could use it to call his 'Daddy'. Igor knew exactly which buttons to press and chatted to Roy for several minutes. Typical of how he wins over strangers was when he met a 50-year old bachelor who almost prides himself on his lack of rapport with or interest in children. Half an hour after their meeting, the pair were engaged in a full-scale battle in Victor's garden. The man lay on the garden path, peppering the tiny boy with imaginary sub-machine-gun fire, while Igor crept up on him with Action Man and a large stick. Gales of childish laughter filtered into the house for the next hour. The man, whom Igor immediately named 'that big giant', was amazed by the boy's agility; Igor reminded him of a baby seal scampering across rocks. He had seen what fun children could be.

Igor is awaiting his new arm, which is a lightweight but slightly longer version that will match his natural arm. The new limb is the one designed specifically for school. He is also due to receive his third pair of custom-built boots. One will be a size eight and the other a nine, to accommodate the super-long big toe that is forcing his foot out at an awkward angle. Barbara is trying to encourage Igor to avoid coasting along on his push car because he needs to build up the muscles in his legs. He is happy at William Cobbett County Junior School, where he will remain until he is eleven years old, but in the next few years Victor will have to carefully consider Igor's future education. He hopes to send him to a school where he can retain the independence that has so far been the key to his success. Victor hopes Igor will want to go on to university, and Barbara expects his future career lies in the world of computing or languages. Igor goes riding every Friday and swimming on Wednesdays. He is a Cub Scout and has been camping with his pack. He continues to ignore the physical differences between himself and other children, but there is an inescapable contrast: Igor faces an uncertain future. The top part of his little body is growing, but not the bottom half, except for the unlikely toe, which resembles ET's finger. Doctors are considering the possibility that Igor may need to use artificial legs as a teenager, but to do this they would have to amputate his small feet. This would be a momentous decision for Igor and one the surgeons won't ask him to make until he is at least thirteen years old and mature enough to consider the consequences. Puberty will be a difficult enough time for Igor and it is then that his awareness of his own physical limitations will be most acute. Should lower-limb surgery be unsuccessful, he will have sacrificed the mobility he already has. If it works, however, artificial legs would increase his height and make him appear better proportioned, although it would be too ambitious for the doctors to increase his height to what is normal for his age. Unfortunately there is a chance that as he grows, the bottom half of his body may be unable to support the top, and therefore his mobility will be threatened. Consequently, Igor's medical team will monitor the development of his pelvis over the next few years. If they judge it able to support the weight of Igor's growing torso this will determine his future treatment. What no doctor has yet told him is that there is a chance he may need to use a wheelchair in his adult life. For someone as energetic as Igor, that would be difficult to bear.

There is also the question mark over Igor's future in Britain. Although Home Secretary Michael Howard indicated in his letter to Victor that the application to extend Igor's visa in 1998 would be looked upon favourably, such pledges are not water-tight. Barbara has told Igor that his home is with her and Roy for as long as he wants. Whatever happens, Victor Mizzi will honour his promise to give Igor a future. If the bureaucrats force him to return to Belarus, Victor intends to seek out a caring foster family for his protégé and to try to find out the answers to the nagging, unanswered questions about his identity. One thing is certain, wherever he lives, Igor will continue to inspire devotion in those who care for him.

Igor and his 'mummy' outside their home

78

Introduction to the Updated Edition

Ten years have passed since Igor: The Courage of Chernobyl's Child was first published in the spring of 1996. Igor's future was at the time filled with uncertainty. Would he have to undergo painful surgical procedures as he grew older? Would he decide to use his prosthetic limbs or choose to function without them? Would he have to accept the use of a wheelchair in the future? Even his very future in Britain seemed precarious. Although Victor Mizzi, Igor's Guardian, had received a letter from Michael Howard MP, then Home Secretary, indicating that the application to extend his UK visa in 1998 would be looked upon favourably, no-one could predict the outcome. Of course, Igor was not privy to these concerns. He simply got on with the business of growing up and all the rites of passage that that entails for any young man: homework, exams, sport, friendships, birthday parties, holidays, discovering the opposite sex, learning to drive, looking for work. From childhood, through adolescence and into maturity, his Foster Mother Barbara Bennett has continued to lovingly assist him with the daily business of discovering independence while supporting him through the inevitable knocks and setbacks faced by any maturing boy, as well as those unique to Igor.

Meanwhile, Victor, now in his early-seventies, has worked tirelessly over the past 14 years to give Igor long-term prospects. It has not always been an easy process, but his steely determination runs as deep as his compassion. Victor has spent tens of thousands of pounds in a bid to offer Igor the most secure future possible. At his Charity's ever more busy offices at his home in Haslemere, Surrey, a long shelf in a bookcase is lined with a dozen lever-arch files chronicling his efforts on behalf of the boy who had captured his attention by offering him, with shining eyes, a piece of bread in the children's hospital all those years earlier. Victor's energy and commitment has paid off. Igor Andrevich Pavlovets was first given leave to remain in the UK on 27 March 1998. Then, on 15 December 2003, he was granted British citizenship and a UK passport.

Victor's concern has not only been for Igor's practical welfare, however. While Barbara has given Igor the security of a loving foster home, the tenacious Charity chairman has helped to give Igor an equally important gift: the knowledge that he was very much loved by his birth family and was taken from them against their will. "Until Igor was 12, nothing was known of his birth family or of the circumstances that led to his early life in a children's hospital in Minsk," says Victor. "It was assumed that his mother, unable to cope with her damaged baby, had given him up." And indeed, this is the perspective from which the first edition of the book about Igor was written. The truth turned out to be very different.

Igor is now a man. He will celebrate his nineteenth birthday on 29 March 2006. Among the presents and cards will be those from Belarus, from the mother and father who were forced to give him up at birth, and from the younger brother and sister whom he is gradually getting to know. For, far from giving away their son because they felt unable to cope with his disabilities, Victor's decade of research on Igor's behalf has turned up a much more sinister history, and one with a superlative outcome. Igor and his birth parents were all human casualties of the then Soviet Union's cover-up of the Chernobyl disaster. The truth has proved at times to be a painful discovery for everyone concerned.

Igor was offered the opportunity to be actively involved in this 20th anniversary update of his story, but chose to decline. He says, "I will be interested to read the updated book and what my birth mother has said in it. It will be the final true account for me, but I don't want to be interviewed any more myself. I just want to get on with my life now."

Barbara adds, "Igor was happy for his birth mother to be interviewed for this update because at last he will find out what really happened when he was born, and that is all he has ever really wanted to know. There has been so much speculation in the past."

The following chapters are researched and written with the intention of satisfying Igor's desire for a definitive account of his early history and the roles of those involved in uncovering it.

The Search

The hunt for the truth about Igor's birth parents began in earnest in 1998. Says Victor: "When Igor came to England in 1994, it was thought that his mother had chosen to abandon him, and was perhaps so ill that she had possibly died, and this story was told so many times in the presence of Igor that – like many of us – he had come to believe it. But as the years went by I felt that I should find out the truth. What if Igor's parents were still alive? What if somewhere there were grandparents?" Victor had been responsible for taking Igor from Belarus to the UK. He now felt responsible for researching the truth about his past in the former Soviet Union. "I felt that it would be important emotionally for him to know the truth, because to live with the fact that you have been abandoned is very difficult."

Victor's chances of finding out what had really happened seemed unlikely. In the former Soviet Union, when a child was separated from his parents they were required to sign away their right of parenthood. There was no bureaucratic transparency in the vast Communist country, and, once signed, these records would never have been made public. After Belarus became an independent Republic, following the fall of Communism in 1991, the chances of finding the names of his parents, and tracking them down, seemed nothing short of impossible. However, Victor had made friends in all echelons of Belarussian society, and had earned the respect of many authority figures through his long-term commitment to the country providing respite holidays for children affected by radiation. His friends and acquaintances in the country included cabinet ministers, army generals and, most crucially, a former senior member of the KGB: the Soviet Union's secret police who had once held files on every citizen. "I was used to talking to people in Belarus about Igor as, from time to time, attempts were made by the country's government to return him to Belarus," explains Victor. "But as the authorities respected and even liked me, they always listened to my arguments and I was able to extend his stay in the UK. To play safe, however, I made Igor a Ward of Court in the UK so that he would be protected by our laws and his future would lie outside the jurisdiction of politics."

Victor continued to visit Belarus regularly to maintain his Charity's connections. During these visits he was often invited to dine with his contacts. Dinner in Belarus tends to last for hours as the host proudly rolls out his finest food and encourages a tide of vodka to flow through his guests. Traditional toasts and formal speeches would punctuate the normal flow of conversation, and, with much back-slapping and joke-telling, relationships between those gathered around the table would be sealed. At one evening event in 1998, Victor was seated next to a key Belarussian figure. "I had always spoken about Igor's progress to many of my friends in Belarus, but on this occasion I spoke to this particular person aware that because of his position, he could possibly find out whether Igor's family were still alive. This was during an evening when I have never seen so much vodka flow, and we left it at that, just a conversation."

When Victor returned the UK he followed up the conversation with a fax addressed to his contact:

Could you please try to find out if the parents of Igor Pavlovets are still alive. If the parents are dead, could you see if you can trace the grandparents or any family. Only give the information to me. Obtaining this information is very important.
Yours sincerely,
Victor Mizzi.

A few months later Victor's fax machine whirred into life, as it did countless times a day with the constant administrative detail required to offer international respite holidays to thousands of children a year. The sheet of paper that emerged from the machine was potentially life changing. It said:

Dear Victor,
I am sending you the information about Igor's parents:
Mother – Pavlovets Elena / 26.03.1965
Other children: Daughter Anna – 4 years old
                         Son Alexei – 6 years old
Father – Pavlovets Andre / 10.07.1965
Father lives with his mother and younger brother
Igor's parents are divorced.
All wishes to you and family.

The fax included the name of a village near Minsk where Elena was said to be living with her children.

"It was the news I had longed to hear," says Victor. "Igor's parents were alive and they had gone on to have two more children, a boy and a girl. I phoned Barbara that week to tell her the news." Igor's Foster Mother accepted it in her quiet way before telling Igor what Victor had discovered. "I wanted Barbara to tell Igor the news because she had the day to day care of him, and I knew that this was a very sensitive issue," he explains. Over the course of the next few months, the news appeared to unsettle Igor, perhaps in part because it had also disturbed Barbara. Although she had had years of experience raising foster children, and encouraging meetings between them and their birth parents, she had never before raised a child from the former Soviet Union. "Barbara did at times find it difficult to believe that because Igor was a Ward of Court no-one could interfere and remove him," says Victor. "But Igor was fully protected. I tried my best to reassure her, but she became increasingly apprehensive about the situation. She began to worry that his natural parents might want to claim their son back, but they couldn't do so because of the Wardship. The question of him being taken was never an issue." Perhaps Barbara was worried that Igor would find it difficult to cope with divided loyalties were they to meet? "I don't think so. Igor is absolutely devoted to Barbara, and very loyal," explains Victor.

Victor believes that Igor naturally picked up his Foster Mother's apprehension. "As time went on, some of these anxieties became instilled into Igor, and he began to believe that if he were to meet his real parents, and they wanted him back, then his life in England would be over," remembers Victor. He reassured Igor that the discovery of his natural parents was no threat to his future with Barbara. Even though the discovery of their existence had created difficult emotions, Victor believed that the potential long-term benefits to Igor of knowing more about them could be huge. He needed to investigate further, to try to develop a relationship with the Pavlovets family and to see what their reaction would be to Igor's situation. "To me, it was a question of doing the right thing for Igor," says Victor emphatically. "I felt that he was fully entitled to be given the opportunity to know the truth about his heritage. I certainly did not want him to grow up assuming that his parents did not want him because of his disabilities. If this issue was not resolved, I feared that it would haunt him all his life."

The Birth Family

Victor's first approach towards Igor's mother was extremely tentative. Who knew how she would react to the news that the baby she had possibly chosen to abandon was now a healthy boy of twelve? He considered the issue at length, and discussed it with his trustees, before deciding to initiate the softest possible initial contact. He asked his Belarussian Charity coordinator, Dennis Vystavkina, to contact Elena Pavlovets and issue an invitation for her two other children, Anna and Alexei, to come to the UK for one of the Charity's four-week respite holidays. "We thought that bringing the children over to another part of the country would be a subtle means to make an initial connection with the family," explains Victor. "It would have been a trust-building exercise and would have allowed a rapport between the adults involved to continue to develop naturally. Obviously we would not have told the children the special reason why they had been invited. Although Igor now knew he had a brother and sister it was unlikely they knew anything about him."

It was Dennis's mother, Galina, also working with the Charity in Belarus, who made the phone call inviting Anna and Alexei Pavlovets to the UK. "Unfortunately, Elena declined the invitation stating that her children were healthy and were not affected by radiation," recalls Victor. He slept on the rejected offer for over a year before deciding to try a more direct approach. On 20 October 2000, he wrote a letter that was translated into Russian and sent to Galina Vystavkina with a request that it should be hand-delivered to Igor's mother. Accompanying Victor's letter was a school photograph of Elena's bespectacled 13-year-old son, a typically cheeky smile creasing his face.

Dear Elena Pavlovets,

For a few years I have been thinking of how to make contact with you. Last year I tried to invite your children to England but you declined the invitation. My name is Victor Mizzi and I live in England and help many children from Belarus. I am writing this in private to you and it is difficult to do as I do not want to upset you.

On 29 March 1987 you gave birth to a baby boy who was born deformed due to radiation. You left him in hospital because you felt that they could look after him better than you. You may not even know his name, he is called Igor Pavlovets.

Igor has been in England since 4 January 1994 and he has grown into a boy to be proud of.

He is at school and doing very well. Because of his personality he is well known in England and he will be 14 years old in March 2001.

He knows that his mother is alive and is very pleased. I told him that because his mother loved him very much she asked the baby hospital to look after him as you were not able to do so in Belarus.

Igor now lives with a foster family and I am his Guardian. I shall soon tell him that he has a brother, Alexei, and a sister, Anna.

I am writing to ask if you would like to meet Igor. I know that this will cause you a lot of pain and bring back the past, but I can assure you that you will be very proud of him and him of you.

If you agree to meet Igor I shall pay for your airfare and that of your two other children to come for a holiday in England.

I am sending you a book written about Igor, and a photograph of how he looks now.

I hope that you will agree to meet him.

I wish you and your family well and happiness.

Best wishes,

Victor E. Mizzi.

Victor also asked Galina to tell the family that if they wanted further contact with him he would fly to Belarus to meet them, but to reassure them that he would do nothing further until he heard from them.

Then he sat back and awaited Galina's call.

Elena Pavlovets was in her kitchen one Saturday afternoon in October 2000, when an unfamiliar car pulled up outside and a well-dressed older woman stepped out. Through her window, Elena could see a younger man in the driving seat. Galina introduced herself to Elena as a representative of a charity called Chernobyl Children Life Line, and told Elena that it was she who had phoned her eighteen months earlier offering her children a respite holiday in England. Curious, and naturally hospitable, Elena immediately invited Galina inside. For the next half an hour they talked together about the work of the Charity before Galina gently told Elena the news that was to change her life: her son Igor had been taken to the UK six years earlier by Victor Mizzi, the chairman of CCLL. Victor was doing everything possible to give Igor the best chance in life and had been trying to find his natural parents for many years.

"I gulped in every single word in because I was hungry for every piece of information," recalls Elena, visibly moved by the intensity of the memory. "I was overwhelmed by what I was hearing, and I was just crying and crying. Igor had been taken from me when he was just a few seconds old and I was never allowed to see him again, but there wasn't a day when I hadn't thought about him. I had always felt that he was alive, and I had often wondered what it would be like to have my three children close to us." For the couple were not divorced but had been happily married for 14 years.

"After his birth, my husband Andre and I had tried everything to find our son, but no-one would tell us what had happened to him. He was ours; we had always wanted him. To hear at last that he was safe and well, and that in the future we could prepare our family to meet him…" Her eyes brim with tears. "It was too much to take in. Galina had started the conversation very gently and softly, but it was very strange when someone you have never met before tells you all about your child. It was so unexpected. I couldn't believe we were really talking about our Igor. I felt so many mixed emotions; tears of happiness that at last he had been found, and tears of sorrow that we had failed to find him ourselves, and instead, someone had to find us."

In fact, events had occurred just as Elena had predicted seven years earlier when in 1993 a brief news-story in the Belarus State newspaper had caught the eye of one of Elena's relatives. Translated from an article I had written in the Daily Express, it told how a boy named Igor Pavlovets had been taken for treatment in England from a children's hospital in Minsk, by a charity chairman named Victor Mizzi. An accompanying photograph showed Igor's excited little face beaming at all the presents that were waiting for him when he arrived at Victor and his wife Birgitta's home. "The relative brought the newspaper to my house and said, 'maybe it is your son'. I looked at the photograph and I was immediately 100 per cent sure it was him," remembers Elena. "There was no doubt in my mind. He looked like us, and although we had not been given the chance to name him, he had our surname. Suddenly, after years of knowing nothing, I learned that he was alive. It was like a light shining through the darkness."

Frustratingly, the translation of the article included scant information; there was nothing to identify the children's hospital in Minsk where Igor had spent the first seven years of his life, and the charity was not named. "All we had was a photograph and the knowledge that he was in England," recalls Elena. "My family had tried to calm me down by saying, 'If he's in England then everything's okay', but it was painful to know that Igor had been living so close by for seven years and despite all our enquiries and efforts to find out what had happened to him, we had not been told. And of course, as the years went by, we'd no way of knowing if Igor was still in England or whether he had returned to Minsk. All we could do from that moment on was live in hope that Igor was going to have a happy life, and that one day he would come looking for us."

And now, just as she had hoped, Igor's envoy was sitting in front of her. Elena remembers telling Galina that she blamed herself for not trying harder to find Igor after she read the newspaper article. "Galina was very reassuring and said I shouldn't blame myself," says Elena. "She reminded me that because of the way our country works that it would have been impossible to find out about anyone in a foreign country. She soothed me, and I felt able to confide in this wise and kind woman."

It was clear that the next step was for Elena and Andre to meet Victor, who would be able to make all the arrangements for them to be reunited with their eldest son, when the time was right. "Galina told me that Victor is a very good and kind man, and immediately I felt very sympathetic towards him because I knew what he had done for our son." Galina then handed Victor's letter to Elena, who says she will never forget the joy of it. "We read every line repeatedly in an attempt to retrieve any additional information about Igor's family life with Barbara and Roy, the good progress he was making in his studies and in sport". At last she was in direct touch with the man who had saved her son, and who was the link to meeting Igor again. The letter calmed her and gave her great hope for the future. "I knew that we would meet Victor, and one day Igor. I didn't know how it would happen but I felt certain that it would. I needed some time to get things straight in my head before I met Victor, but I trusted that things would happen as Galina had said. I was hungry for contact to be established as soon as possible."

As soon as Andre came home, Elena told him all that had happened. That night, memories of the past came flooding back. The story of how Elena came to absorb the radiation that meant she would be denied a life with her first-born child is deeply disturbing. That her life with Andre should have taken such a tragic turn is particularly upsetting given their devoted history together and the fact that their baby was planned and very much wanted. In 2006 they celebrate their 20th wedding anniversary, just nine weeks before that of the world's worst nuclear disaster.

"I grew up in the same village as Andre's grandmother, about half an hour from Minsk. Andre and I met when we were 14 years old and we have been together ever since," says Elena proudly. "When he did his military service he was sent to an Army camp near Moscow for two years and we wrote to each other constantly while he was away; sometimes I received three letters a week from him, and we met up once or twice in that time." When Andre returned home from military service the young couple were married. The date was 22 February 1986. They were both aged 22. The wedding photographs show a serious young bride in a traditional white dress uncertain about being the centre of attention as she commits herself to her handsome, besuited Andre.

Two months later, Chernobyl reactor number four exploded over the border in Ukraine and became the most radioactive place on earth. The newly wed couple, like most other people in the Soviet Union, were told nothing. Instead, they continued to focus on the details of their new life together. Andre had started a new job working at the communal farm near their village, and Elena was completing her final year of an agriculture degree at Grodno University, 300 km west of Minsk, near the border with Poland. They met when they could. "We had always planned to have children and we wanted a large family," says Elena. "So I was overjoyed when in August, six months after our wedding, I found I was pregnant. Looking back, I was so calm about it all. I was just naturally confident that everything would happen the way it was supposed to." A few weeks later, however, the agricultural student received a government directive ordering her to leave university for three months and take up a job at a communal farm in Mstislavl, in the south-east of Belarus, on the border with Ukraine. State control was everything in the USSR at that time, and Elena was unable to simply refuse the directive. The farm to which she was being sent by the Communist authorities lay just 50 miles from the stricken Chernobyl reactor. She had no idea that on 26 April 1986, just three months before Igor was conceived, that a reactor there had melted down with terrible, invisible consequences, and that the farm to which she was being sent now lay in the most contaminated area. Just five months earlier, a lethal cloud of radioactive dust had been released from the explosion and was working its deadly way into the food chain.

The Republic of Belarus eventually received an estimated 70 per cent of the entire nuclear fallout from the Ukrainian reactor because of the way the wind was blowing – directly towards the farm where Elena had been sent to work. The land was showered with radioactive isotopes. Everything the mother-to-be ate while she was there and everything she touched was endangering her unborn child. "I was sent to that area for three months in September 1986," she recalls, bitterly. "The authorities told us nothing. We heard rumours that people had been advised to stay indoors for a few days because there had been a problem at a power plant in Ukraine, but we didn't know why. I wasn't given a choice about whether to go there or not, and we weren't told how serious the problem had been. I had no idea that the area to which I had been sent had already become one of the most heavily contaminated areas. I was unaware that living and working there could damage my health. How could something that had happened 50 miles away possibly damage me or my child?"

It was only when she was briefly shown her newborn baby that she began to draw her own conclusions. On 29 March 1987, a year and three days after the Chernobyl catastrophe, Igor was born. "I wasn't worried about anything during my pregnancy because I had no need to be. Although there were no ultrasound diagnostics, the doctors could hear with a stethoscope that everything sounded quite normal," she recalls.

I ask what plans she had made for her new life with her first baby. "My plans at that time? My plans were to give birth to a child and take him home and bring him up." Her blue eyes redden.

Elena's labour lasted more than a day and required no intervention. At that time, doctors in the USSR did not allow fathers to be present at the birth of their children, and they did not hand babies to their mothers directly after birth, as they do now. Instead, new babies were shown briefly to their mothers before being taken away for tests and on to the hospital nursery for 24 hours before being returned for the first feed. Elena didn't expect to be able to hold her newborn baby until the following day, but neither did she expect the casual brutality of what she was told a few minutes after giving birth. "The baby didn't cry, so the first sound I heard was the doctor speaking. He said, 'You have given birth to something unusual, he is something like a piece of flesh'." The doctor placed the tiny newborn baby on his flat palm and showed him quickly to his mother. She was able to look at him for just a few seconds.

"Although it was an immediate and devastating emotion when I saw his handicap, I loved him immediately," she says. "But because he didn't cry I didn't know if he was alive or dead, and no-one told me. Two or three seconds was all I was given to look at him, so I didn't even have a chance to see clearly which limbs he had and which he hadn't." After those brief seconds, when Igor was shown dismissively to his distraught mother, he was taken away. It was to be the first and last time she would see him for sixteen years.

"I never even held him," she says quietly, wiping away tears. "Normally a newborn baby would be brought to the mother after a day for feeding. But for the two days after Igor was born there was no information at all about what was happening and no one brought him to me. I was panicking with the stress of it all and I can't remember what happened in that time." Forty-eight hours after the birth, a professor came and interviewed Elena for an hour-and-a-half. "He

89

quizzed me, asking whether I had smoked or drunk while I was pregnant. After his questions he said that there was no way the baby could survive and that they would not give him to me. I broke down then. At the end of the interview I mentioned that I had been to the Chernobyl zone. As soon as he heard that, he told me to keep my mouth shut and not tell anyone else. If Igor was alive I wanted to take him back to our home and look after him, whatever the prognosis, but I wasn't allowed to see him again. There was no more information."

At the time of Igor's birth, the Communist government of the then USSR claimed that children 'belonged' to the State. In consequence, a child born disabled like Igor immediately became the State's property and bureaucrats would determine what happened to him. Government policy dictated that parental rights over Igor were removed at birth. This attitude prevailed until the fall of Communism and the break-up of the Soviet Union, when Igor was four. Because Andre wasn't permitted to attend the birth, he never even saw his first-born child. "Andre was at home waiting for news of the birth," explains Elena. "When no news came he visited the hospital to try and see us, but no one would let him in after Igor was born." Frantic with worry, Andre shouted up to Elena's room on the second floor, a few hours after the professor's visit. The couple could communicate only through the window. "I told him that we didn't have a baby, and that I would tell him why when I came home. I told him that I didn't want anyone to visit me, I wanted to be alone."

On 10 April 1987, 12 days after the birth, Elena was finally discharged. Before she left there was one further brutality. "I was given something to sign, but I didn't even read it. I was left in such a bad psychological condition that I didn't care about anything at that time." This document has also emerged through Victor's research and last year, for the first time since she signed it, Elena was given a copy. Translated into English the handwritten record says:

10 April 1987
I am Elena Pavlovets refusing my child born on 29 March, 1987, in Minsk. Signed: Elena Pavlovets.

There is also an identical document in the same handwriting, signed by Igor's father. Over the coming weeks, Elena and Andre kept trying to find out what had happened to their son. "Twice we went to the hospital and asked for any information about our baby, but the officials said they didn't know anything. On the second visit they denied I had even given birth there and made it clear we shouldn't come back again. Everywhere was a red light. Was he alive or had he

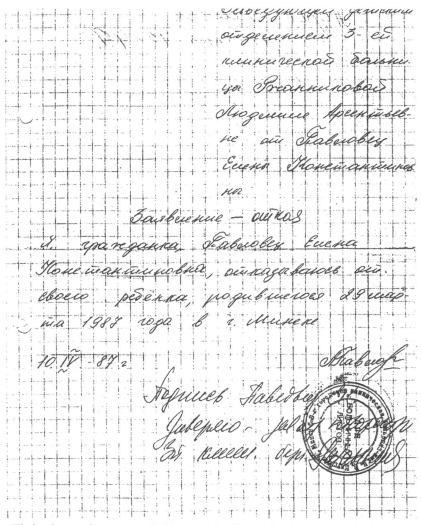

The handwritten document in which Igor's mother Elena is forced to sign away her baby boy.

died? No answers were ever given. The emotional stress was so great that for a significant time I could not function. During the next year, before I conceived our second child, I remember nothing but empty space inside my soul." During this time, Andre calmly supported his wife with tenderness and understanding. "Sometimes, in other families, men leave when such things happen, but Andre stayed and looked after me all the time," says Elena. "When we were trying without success to find out information about Igor, and nothing worked out, Andre was always there, helping me to calm down and reassuring me that everything would happen as it should. I am very lucky to have him. He helped me a lot during that year."

Although the couple were afraid of having other children, they were now desperate to try for another baby. "It was very frightening to give birth to my next child, but I wanted a baby more than anything after I lost Igor," explains Elena. "I just had to take it as it was and wait until the baby was born." Fortunately, throughout her second pregnancy, Elena received close medical supervision. "They felt the baby before he was born to make sure that his limbs were all there, and ran other tests." Alexei was born on the 25 March 1989, four days before Igor's second birthday. "When Alexei was born he was crying very loudly so I immediately knew that everything was alright this time. As soon as I felt him within my arms I loved him more than life itself. A mother usually loves her children, but after what had happened it made my love even stronger," explains Elena. Twenty-two months later, on 21 January 1991, the couple's equally adored daughter Anna was born – eleven months before the collapse of the Soviet Union. "The births of my second and third children helped to fill the empty space in my soul, but very often, when all the family were gathering at the table for example, I would look sadly and think that there should be one more child sitting there," Elena explains, rubbing away tears. "I was always remembering Igor, and thinking that he should be with the four of us. It's very hard to take when you lose your first baby and don't know what has happened to him."

Although they now had two healthy children, Elena and Andre continued to make enquiries as the years went by about the fate of the baby son they could not forget. "We asked questions but there were never any answers," recalls Elena. "People told us not to bother to ask. Everything was kept like a secret. We were unable to find out anything." It wasn't until 1993, six years after Igor's birth, that she first heard news about her eldest child when her relative spotted the article stating that a boy named Igor Pavlovets had been taken to England for medical treatment. It caused a tumult of emotion for Elena. "The article brought all my feelings about losing Igor back to the surface. I was very distraught until my second child was born, and Alexei's birth helped me to cope with losing my first baby. By the time Anna was born I was even starting to forget some of the difficult emotions. Everyone had always been careful not to talk about Igor to me; they didn't want to damage me because they knew how painful it had been for me. But now, with the article, it all came flooding back." However, she was still unable to contact her son because the article did not mention the charity's name. All she had was a name: Victor Mizzi. This was a pre-Internet age and although Belarus had now become an independent Republic it was still impossible to seek such information.

What action would Elena and Andre have taken had there had been an address for the Charity in the newspaper article? "We would have investigated to see what the benefits were of him going to the UK, and I expect that we would then have explored further the possibility of him coming back to live with his family on his return." Elena is aware this might have been difficult. "We had no documents, no evidence, nothing to prove that he really was our son." She had nothing, in fact, apart from the life-enhancing knowledge that her baby had survived, despite the professor's brutal prognosis. "I felt confident that Igor would have good prospects in life in England, but I didn't expect to hear about him again," she admits.

Another six years passed. Then, one day, Elena's phone rang. "A lady introduced herself and said that Anna and Alexei had been invited to the UK by a British charity for a holiday to help them recuperate from the effects of radiation," remembers Elena. "I thought it was a mistake; I knew that there were children much worse off who were living in the contaminated area. My children lived in Minsk and were perfectly healthy. I thanked the lady for her interest and put the phone down." Moments later, she froze. "I suddenly wondered if this call could have had something to do with Igor. I began to think about the connection between the article mentioning Igor was England, and now a British charity calling me. I was knocked out by the call, and I immediately regretted my hasty reaction, for I had no means of getting back in touch with the caller to see if this charity had anything to do with Victor Mizzi, a name I had never been able to forget." She often thought about the call and whether she had just passed up her only chance to find out more about Igor. But perhaps it really was just a coincidence. She had no way of finding out. Another 18 months were to pass before she would get a second chance and Galina arrived with her bombshell. "I realise now why Victor was taking things cautiously," says Elena. "I can see now that he was thinking of the best way of contacting us and telling us about Igor. Once he sent Galina to see me everything began to fall in to place, she won our trust and we became very good friends. When Galina told me that Igor was still in England and was making a life there, we were very glad because in Belarus he wouldn't have had the opportunities. But we were also angry about what had happened. To think that for seven years Igor had been in Minsk so close to our home … and that no-one gave us any information to help us find our son … If it wasn't for Victor Mizzi we would never have found him."

The Reunion

Victor was half way through an ordinary day working for Chernobyl Children Life Line. He had issued a batch of letters inviting a group of new children to come to the UK for a respite holiday, he had sorted out a few problems connected to children already here, and he had dealt with some of the endless paperwork concerning the laundry block that the charity has built in the deprived Belarussian village of Lapitchy. The phone rang and Victor absentmindedly picked it up.

"Hello?" he said.

"Hello Victor, this is Galina. I have some news for you. Elena Pavlovets would like to meet you," she said. Victor was jubilant. "Galina had won their confidence and had worked very hard with the family," says Victor, who had sensed from the start that it was important to have a Belarussian citizen involved with the family because they would understand each other's mentality. "I felt great satisfaction. For the first time I could see a light at the end of the tunnel for Igor to meet his birth parents. At that stage I thought it would be an easy process," he says. "I had no idea then of the problems we were to encounter before this meeting would take place."

Elena had elected to meet Victor in Minsk, rather than in her village, half an hour to the east of the capital. "I was sensitive to their situation," says Victor. "And I understood that it was important for them to keep me at arm's length so that they would not become the object of gossip in their small village. I was to meet them in Minsk, in the square outside the Roman Catholic Cathedral, and I expected a short initial meeting." It was a bitterly cold winter's day when Victor and Dennis made their way in the charity's minibus to the Cathedral. The date was 13 January 2001. Standing at the edge of the square were two ladies warmly dressed in winter coats and mink hats waiting nervously in the chill air. They were Elena Pavlovets and her husband's aunt, Larissa, whom she had brought with her for support. "We chose that place because it was important for us to keep the meeting private," explains Elena, who says she felt very worried before she met Victor for the first time. "I wondered what words to use and what to ask him. I felt a bit overwhelmed by all the confusing feelings and thoughts." Inevitably, it was a highly charged meeting. "We introduced ourselves, and started talking with great emotion," remembers Victor. Tears drenched Elena's face as she spoke. Victor could tell immediately that she was a very sincere and intelligent person. "She was weeping throughout, and I could feel the pain that she had suffered, even though 13 years had passed," he says. "She told me that there was not a single day when she had not thought of Igor. She told me that she had been a young woman when her baby was taken away from her, only moments after his birth; she had not known if he were alive or dead. She struck me as someone who was still extremely disturbed by what had happened. Her love and care for her child was evident. She wanted to know everything about Igor, his health, where he was living, about his education. She wanted as much information about him as she could get." So Victor told them all about Igor, about his courage, his good looks and his happy life in Britain.

"I asked many questions," recalls Elena. "I was hungry for information and wanted to know every single detail about my son. I was also very interested to find out how Victor was able to take Igor to the UK because I knew that it was very difficult at that time to take a disabled child out of the country." Elena was equally curious about Victor's first meeting with Igor. Why had he chosen to help her son when there were so many other children also in need of assistance? She says, "Even before we met Victor he was already very dear to us – words of gratitude don't begin to express our feelings about what he has done for Igor – and it was important to me to know why he had done it." Victor told Elena the story about how Igor had pulled off a piece of his bread and offered it to him. "So this was how he got into his heart," says Elena. "No-one could fail to be moved by that situation. I was amazed by Igor's character. I will remember this story forever, and I am proud of him." At last, after so many years, she had an insight into her child's personality.

"Elena told me that she had a good family and a very good, loving husband," recalls Victor. "She explained that Andre, her husband, was working at the tractor factory in Minsk, and that he was very anxious and concerned to know what was happening and that she wanted to take me to meet him. The bonding between us was evident," he recalls. The four-strong party immediately set off for the tractor factory, in the industrial area of Minsk, in the charity's minibus. Victor and Dennis waited while Elena went inside before reappearing with her husband, a tall, slim, good-looking man in his late thirties with bright blue eyes like his aunt Larissa, and sporting a neat brown moustache. "He was very dignified and quiet, and greeted me with affection," recalls Victor. "He was clearly full of pride in the news of his son, and gave me a bear-hug in greeting." Elena and Andre conversed quietly in Russian, before Elena turned to Dennis and issued an astonishingly trusting invitation. "Elena said that Andre had invited us home with them to meet their other two children, and to see where they lived, which was about half an hour's drive from Minsk in a typical country village," recalls Victor. "He trusted me and he wanted, very proudly, to show me his home and to meet his much-loved family. Andre may say very little, but he is a calming factor in the family. When Elena was crying, he would point out that they should be happy because Igor was healthy and being well looked after."

By the time the charity's minibus crunched along the frozen road leading into the small rural village, it was nearly dark. Light from simple wooden cottages spilled on to thick snow outside. Victor saw that the Pavlovets' house was unusual for the area, in that it was constructed of brick, not timber. It had a tall brick chimney and a concrete porch. Elena explained to Victor proudly that it was all her husband's work and that he was building a new floor upstairs. The couple then took Victor and Dennis on a tour of their home. "We were shown Andre's workshop, their dog, their milk cows and their plot for growing vegetables for their winter food," says Victor, "And all the time Elena was talking of how she had never, for a single day, forgotten about her eldest son and had continually wondered what had happened to him."

Because Igor's brother and sister did not know that they had an elder brother, Victor and Dennis were introduced as family friends. No foreigners had ever been to the village before and the children were intrigued by the non-Russian speaker in their midst. Eleven-year-old Alexei was quite reserved but seemed passionate about the motorbike he was reconditioning in his father's workshop. Ten-year old Anna, a talented artist who proudly showed the visitors her paintings and drawings, was outgoing and talkative. She was also the mirror image of Igor at the same age, and shared with her unknown brother the same intelligent gaze and fine features. After an hour and a half, it was time to leave. Later that night, back in his Minsk hotel room, Victor felt profoundly satisfied by the experience of meeting Elena and Andre, and hopeful about helping Igor to develop a relationship with them in the future. "I knew that this was the best thing I could have done for Igor, but it was also clear to me that it would be very good for his family too. These good, honest people still suffered the consequences of having their eldest child removed from their lives. Discovering what had happened to the son they had never wanted to give up was important for their emotional welfare as well." Victor believed strongly that a meeting would benefit both child and parents.

On his return to the UK a few days later, Victor immediately invited Barbara and her thirteen-year-old foster son to his home to tell them all about his visit. Firstly, he showed Igor the photographs he had taken of his family; his little sister Anna in a green jumper clutching her doll; his father Andre in his fur collar looking intently at the camera; his younger brother Alexei standing in the snow; and his mother Elena clutching photographs of him, her unknown yet unforgettable son. "I talked to Igor about his family, and he was very interested in them, asking questions and showing a lot of interest in both his brother and sister, as well as his mother and father." Victor also read Igor a letter that he had written for the boy about the meeting before handing it to him to keep. "I wanted Igor to have an accurate record of my visit and the truth about why he had been forced to spend his early years in institutional care."

Dear Igor,

I met your mother on the 13 January 2001, together with your Aunty Larissa who is your father's sister.

Your mother Elena is 37 years old and her birthday is on the 26 March. She lives in a village with your father Andre who is 37 years old, your brother Alexei and your sister Anna.

When you were born it was a very different country to what it is now. It was the USSR and people had to do what they were told, also the people of the USSR could not travel or move from one region to another as the secret police controlled everyone.

On the 26 April 1986 there was a big explosion in the Chernobyl nuclear plant. The USSR did not want the world to know that radiation had killed many people and that babies were being born deformed. At that time no one could travel to the USSR.

When you were in your mother's tummy, the doctors told her that there were no problems, but when you were born you had no arm and small feet, you also had a lot of 'radiation spots' on your body.

The doctors told your mother that you only had a few days to live and on the second day after you had been born they made your parents sign some papers and then took you away.

Your parents did not have any choice in this and they were very sad and upset. No matter how hard they tried they could not find out where you were or even if you were alive.

Then all of a sudden what was known as Communism collapsed, and Belarus, your country, was no longer a part of the USSR and people were allowed to go to Belarus and news of the explosion started to become known.

I found you at the end of 1992, you were in the baby hospital and Tamara Mouroshava was looking after you on the top floor.

You were very special, but were with a lot of deformed and sick children. Tamara used to take you back to her home for weekends and she loved you very much.

It took me one-and-a-half years to obtain a permit and visa for you to come to England and you were only to come for three months, and from now on you know the story.

Now, about your family:

When I talked to your Mum and Aunty, your Mum was crying all the time, not because she was sad but because she was happy that you are alive and doing well in England. You also have grandparents and cousins.

Your father works at a tractor factory in Minsk and goes home at weekends. He is very tall and handsome and you look very much like him. He works very hard.

Alexei, your brother, is 11 years old and his birthday is on the 25 March. He looks like you. He has a tractor and helps on the farm. He has an old car and is working on it at the moment.

Your sister Anna is very pretty and is nine years old. Both your brother and sister are very polite and friendly.

They live in a village and they have a very nice home, which your father has worked on, a garage with a tractor and a shed that houses a big cow.

The house is very clean and it has a hall, bathroom, toilet, sitting room and one bedroom which Alexei and Anna share, and another for your parents.

Your father is now building a further floor above the house.

You have inherited the Pavlovets' courage and spirit and your family are so happy for you and would like to see you in England when you are ready.

As I said to you, I am your Guardian and no one is going to take you away, nor does anyone want to take you away.

Your mother was very pleased with the photograph that I gave her of you and she was going to tell your brother and sister about you.

I suggest that you put the photographs of your family in your room and be very proud of your country and your family.

Victor Mizzi, Guardian.

At Victor's suggestion, copies of the letter connecting Igor to his past were sent to the office of the Official Solicitor, as well as to the Psychiatrist appointed by the court to work with Igor, and from whom Victor had been taking advice, determined not to do any damage to Igor by his enquiries. Although the meeting between Victor, Igor and Barbara appeared to have gone well, the discovery of Igor's natural parents caused deep emotions to surface, and was to lead to powerful differences of opinion about how best to handle Igor's future. Victor, his legal Guardian, felt that a meeting between Igor and his parents was in Igor's best interests, and that it should happen sooner rather than later. "One never knows what the future holds, or what might happen to Igor or to his parents," he says. "I felt that there was no time to lose." He discussed the situation at length with his charity's trustees, drawing on their combined wealth of knowledge, and he also had a number of private meetings with the Psychiatrist appointed by the Wardship Court. "There was a team within the charity who were involved in thinking through what would be best for Igor's future; it wasn't a one-man operation. It was very important that I was doing the right thing, I am very self critical in these things, and they were my check, as was the Psychiatrist. We all had to work out what was best for Igor."

Barbara, Igor's devoted Foster Mother, was equally motivated by the desire to do what she thought was best for Igor, but her eventual position was that she was reluctant to encourage a meeting between Igor and his natural parents until Igor was 18, another five years away. "There was also an underlying fear that she would lose him, that his parents – or his country – would want to take him back," says Victor, who reminded Barbara that Igor was in no danger of being forced back to Belarus against his will: the Wardship protected him. Furthermore, Victor would not have gone ahead if he was in any doubt about the intentions of Igor's natural parents. "Elena and Andre were relieved that their son was in England, where he could get all the medical attention he needed and which they could not provide," asserts Victor. "Andre had urged Elena to 'be happy that he is alive', and it was an appropriate sentiment." They also respected the strong bond of love that had developed between Barbara and Igor. "Tearing them apart was not their intention, they simply wanted the chance to take up my invitation to meet him." Igor's life in the UK was managed by a complicated set of legal and emotional relationships and it had at times proved difficult for all parties to work in harmony together. Sadly, at no time was this truer than over discussions about a possible meeting with his birth parents. Divided loyalties placed Igor in a difficult situation. He did not want to seem disloyal to Barbara, the surrogate mother who had given him so much since he was a little boy overwhelmed by his arrival in a new country. He dealt with the situation by becoming dismissive whenever his natural parents were discussed, something that none of the adults in his life wanted.

"He would refer to his parents by saying, 'They are just people'," recalls Victor. "I felt he needed encouragement and support to find the confidence to meet them. But as time went on he became more and more adamant that his parents didn't matter to him. I didn't feel that this was a particularly healthy response. My belief, and that of my advisors, was that Igor would find a meeting easier and more beneficial than he appeared to imagine." Victor was convinced that the meeting would be a source of healing for Igor, and that although it might be difficult for the adults involved, that the child's needs had to take precedence. "My belief is that we do not own our children, whether they are ours by blood or through our decision to care for them," says Victor. "The interests of the child should always be paramount." And so he decided to take legal advice. "I've known many children from Belarus who have been permanently removed from their family, and it is always of great concern to them. Having some contact with their natural parents helps all children immensely. I was convinced that giving Igor the opportunity to meet his family would enable him to face his future life secure in the knowledge that he was not abandoned as a baby."

But obstacles to the meeting continued to emerge. "Following my initial suggestion that Igor meet his parents, the Official Solicitor was positive to the extent that he would ask *when* Igor was going to meet his parents," recalls Victor. "Unfortunately, it seemed as if Igor's Social Worker was then persuaded by other adults in Igor's life that the meeting should not happen, and, eventually, Social Services then enlisted the support of the Official Solicitor." A seemingly insurmountable division had now emerged as Victor found himself battling against all other parties in Igor's life. "The opposition to the meeting grew stronger as time went by and I had many clashes with all parties, in particular with Social Services whom I thought were wrong in trying to prevent this boy from meeting his parents." Regrettably, Igor overheard some telephone disputes about his future and was no doubt unsettled when he saw that his Foster Mother was becoming upset. It was an all too easy step for him to conclude that Victor was no longer on his side. However, fuelled by a conviction that he was doing what was right for Igor's long-term future, and undaunted by the battery of objection building up against him, Victor took his only chance and engaged a firm of Solicitors, Reynolds, Porter and Chamberlain, to take the matter to the Wardship Court to obtain definitive judgement. His dedicated Solicitor, Carolynn Usher, was as determined as Victor to help give Igor a real choice about meeting his parents. It was not a quick or a cheap process, although given the nature of the case the Solicitors reduced their fees to their bare minimum, despite the hundreds of hours of work involved. The case dragged on for nearly two years, and involved a leading QC. "These things are expensive, but you've got to do them," says Victor who made many appearances at court.

Meanwhile, in Belarus, Elena Pavlovets was beginning to prepare her two youngest children for a possible future meeting with Igor. "I didn't tell the children straight away that they had an older brother," she says. "They were still young and I didn't want it to be too great a shock. I had to find the right words to gently introduce the subject." When Alexei was 12 and Anna was 10, Elena decided they were ready. "I didn't tell them everything in one go, it was step by step," she recalls. "I explained that before they were born I had had another baby who was so small that the doctors couldn't even say it was a real person when they looked at him, and that because of this they had taken the baby from me in the hospital. The children immediately asked me why the baby had been taken, and I told them that I didn't know myself." She added that the baby had grown into a happy boy being looked after by kind people in England, who were doing everything to give him a good life. She decided not to mention that he had been living close by in Minsk before he went to England. "That was not an important thing for them to know," she explains. "I was afraid that if they knew he had been in Minsk they would ask why we hadn't visited them, and it was too difficult to explain. I didn't want them to mix up thoughts in their heads and I didn't want them to worry; I wanted to protect them from bad feelings and thoughts, so I kept the two worlds separate." The children accepted the news calmly. "They said that they were glad they had an older brother," says Elena.

In 2001, at the suggestion of the court-appointed Psychiatrist, Victor made a videotape of Igor's birth family and showed it to Igor. "He watched with a smile on his face, and was very inquisitive," recalls Victor. "I made it clear to him that it was his choice as to when he would meet them." Soon, presents and letters were travelling in both directions. The Psychiatrist's report suggested that Igor did not currently have the emotional strength to cope with meeting them in person yet, although he concluded, 'Mr Mizzi and [myself] both understand that Igor is curious. His willingness to exchange letters, presents and videotapes with his birth family show that Igor is moving towards opening the door further, in his imagination, to direct contact starting.'

Early the following year, Victor wrote a letter to Igor:

'[Yesterday] we spoke about your parents and also about your country and I can understand your concerns of being afraid and having butterflies in your tummy. Although you say that they are just people, they are your mum and dad who love you and are proud of you. As I said, when you eventually meet them you will wonder why you were ever worried...I assure you that your parents will never ask to take you back as your life is here in England with us...You have great courage and I am very proud of you, you always see the funny side of life.'

By May 2002, the Psychiatrist involved in the case had observed significant positive changes in Igor. "Igor has gained from learning about his birth family in Belarus," he wrote in a letter to Victor's Solicitor, Carolynn Usher. During the intricate case, Victor was aware that valuable months were being lost to Igor and his parents, and then he was informed that there was to be a change of Official Solicitor. "He was a breath of fresh air," he recalls. "He was genuinely interested in the long-term interest of the child. He was a person I found I could communicate clearly with, and together we were able to show a united front to the Judge. Things began to move quickly from that point on." It had taken the best part of two years but on 7 May 2003 Mr Justice Singer was able to make a consent order enabling the contact to take place. It was now considered in sixteen-year-old Igor's best interests to meet his birth parents. The tenacious charity chairman had achieved a remarkable victory for Igor and his birth family. "I knew that there was still a chance that he would refuse to see his parents," says Victor, "But that had never been grounds for not trying to do the best for him. I set out by bringing Igor to England to help him, and I take my responsibilities seriously." The Judge instructed a child psychiatrist to prepare Igor for the meeting, and asked Victor to make all the necessary arrangements for the reunion to take place. "I did have an extremely large bill in legal fees, but it was something that had to be done," insists Victor. "It must have been a terrible feeling for Igor to think that his parents did not want him. Now he could find out the truth for himself." Although Igor's initial attitude towards having contact with his natural family had been ambivalent, his view shifted over the course of time, just as Victor had predicted. On 21 June 2003, Elena and Andre Pavlovets and their children Alexei, 14, and 12-year-old Anna, boarded an aeroplane for the first time in their lives, en route to meet Igor – the missing fifth member of their family.

Igor was just a few minutes old when she last saw him. Now, 16 years later and in another world, Elena Pavlovets and her son were at last reunited in an English village. It was an extraordinary and poignant meeting. Elena had loved her baby fiercely from the moment she first saw him, but although their bond had been cruelly broken she never gave up hope of seeing her son again.

Childhood sweethearts: Elena Valencova and Andre Pavlovets take their wedding vows on 22 February 1986, just two months before the disaster at the Chernobyl power station. They had been together since they were both 14 years old.

Just married: Elena and Andre Pavlovets begin a new life together, supported by family and friends.

Devastation: Elena and Andre photographed in 1988, a year after Igor's birth. They were desperate to find out what had happened to their first baby, and to conceive another child.

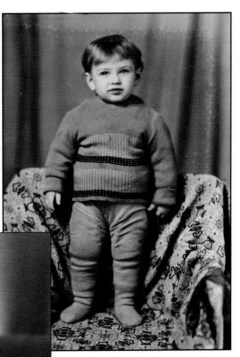

Igor's father, Andre Pavlovets, at the age of 18 months.

A brave boy: Igor Andrevich Pavlovets in 1989, aged two-and-a-half.

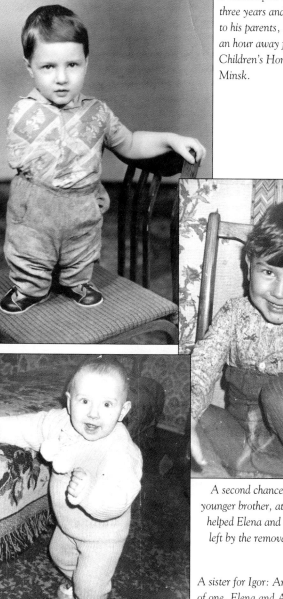

Dressed up in his best clothes: Igor aged three years and five months. Unknown to his parents, he was living only half an hour away from their village, at Children's Home Number One in Minsk.

A second chance: Alexei Pavlovets, Igor's younger brother, at the age of two. His birth helped Elena and Andre fill the terrible gap left by the removal of Igor from their lives.

A sister for Igor: Anna Pavlovets at the age of one. Elena and Andre's family was now complete, but they always felt the absence of their first-born.

Our little boy: Alexei Pavlovets, aged four, and looking very much like his elder brother.

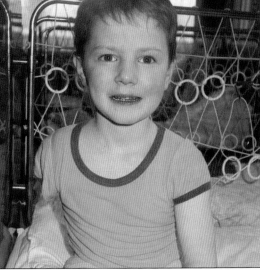

My cot: Six-year-old Igor in the children's hospital in April 1993, a few hours after Victor Mizzi, the Chairman of Chernobyl Children Life Line met him for the first time.

Igor, aged six, with his treasured toy fire engine donated by **Daily Express** *reader, Vic Tucker.*

Igor with Victor on the day after he arrived in England, on 5 January, 1994.

Picture: Express Newspapers

Trying on his bionic arm and his elevated boots for the first time, with prosthetist Alan Stephenson.

Picture: Barry Gomer, Express Newspapers

Igor's smiling face shows his excitement at having the arm about which he had dreamed.

Picture: Barry Gomer, Express Newspapers

Igor practising to be a fireman on his climbing frame in the Bennett's garden.

Picture: Larry Ellis, Express Newspapers

Watch me fly!

Picture: Larry Ellis, Express Newspapers

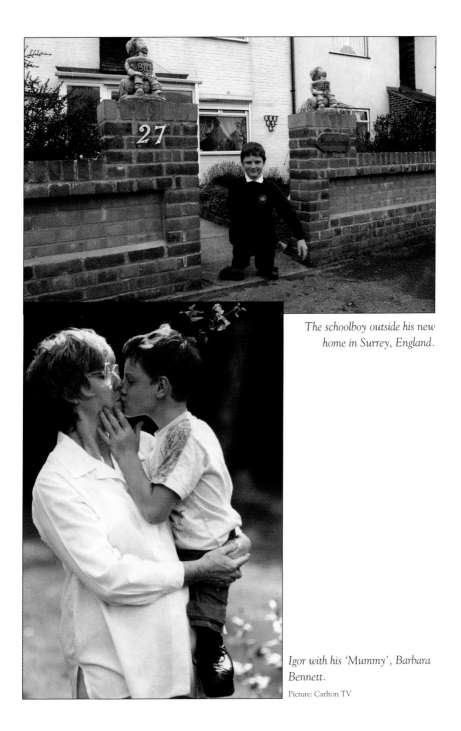

The schoolboy outside his new home in Surrey, England.

Igor with his 'Mummy', Barbara Bennett.

Picture: Carlton TV

Igor makes another friend.

Igor's left arm has always been exceptionally strong, and his determination to try anything means that his personality seems to overwhelm his disability.

The first photograph that Igor saw of his mother Elena and father Andre taken a few hours after Victor met them for the first time on 13 January 2001.

A brother for Igor: Eleven-year-old Alexei Pavlovets, the first time Victor met him.

Igor's younger sister Anna, aged ten, at home in Belarus.

Our son: A school photograph of thirteen-year-old Igor sits in pride of place in his parents' bedroom near Minsk. It would be another three years before they were to be reunited with their son.

Igor, aged thirteen, six weeks before Victor met his birth parents for the first time.

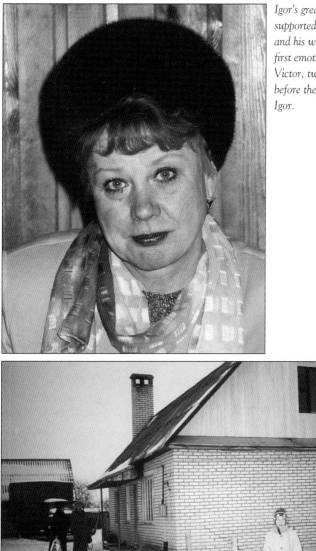

Igor's great-aunt Larissa who supported her nephew Andre and his wife Elena during the first emotional meeting with Victor, two-and-a-half years before they were reunited with Igor.

Igor's ten-year-old sister Anna outside her family's village home.

Elena Pavlovets shortly after meeting Victor for the first time.

We did it! Victor Mizzi and Igor prepare to meet Igor's parents at Victor's Surrey home in June 2003.

Picture: Douglas Morrison, Express Newspapers

Andre Pavlovets in 2001, he had never once set eyes upon his eldest son.

A family reunited: (left to right) Igor's parents, Elena Pavlovets and her husband Andre, sixteen-year-old Igor, his twelve-year-old sister Anna, Igor's foster mother Barbara Bennett, and his fourteen-year-old brother Alexei.

Pictures: Douglas Morrison, Express Newspapers

Elena Pavlovets and her son Igor had waited sixteen years to hold each other.

Picture: Douglas Morrison, Express Newspapers

A complete family at last: (left to right) Igor's fourteen-year-old brother Alexei, his mother Elena, Igor, his father Andre, his twelve-year-old sister Anna.

Thirteen-year-old Anna Pavlovets, the year after she met her older brother Igor for the first time. She has become an avid student of English and often sends him letters and cards.

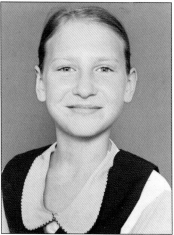

Igor and his father Andre enjoy a tractor ride around Victor's garden together following their first ever meeting in June 2003.

My Mum and Dad.
Picture: Douglas Morrison, Express
Newspapers

Igor, aged eighteen, visits his birth family's home in Belarus for the first time in the summer of 2005: (left to right) Igor's cousin, Igor's fourteen-year-old sister Anna, Igor's foster mother Barbara Bennett, Igor, his father Andre, Igor's cousin.

As soon as Elena was told that Igor and Barbara had just arrived at Victor's house, she rushed to the kitchen door to meet them. "I ran to Igor and I hugged him. Immediately I had the same loving feelings as if I was kissing Anna and Alexei, and I couldn't take my eyes off him," she recalls, crying at the memory. Although face to face with one another again, mother and son were still separated by a language barrier – Elena speaks no English, and Igor no longer remembers his Russian – but this moment was about much more than words. "We don't know what question to ask first," said a trembling Elena at the time, as she gazed with pride at her handsome first-born as he handed gifts to Alexei and Anna. "Such excitement. I am extremely proud seeing him. My expectations have been fulfilled." Both she and Barbara were crying. During their visit, Igor enjoyed a summer barbeque with both his families, and they went to the beach together for a picnic. Victor and his wife Birgitta also gave a garden party at which Igor and his family were able to meet many of those who had been involved in Igor's life in this country.

Elena was struck by the visual similarity between Igor and his sister Anna. "Seeing Igor and Anna sitting together in a restaurant one evening, they looked almost like one person: they have such similar faces." Elena had explained to her two youngest children before they left Minsk that there was something different about Igor's physique. "They didn't take any notice of his disability," says Elena. "It was as if they hadn't even noticed. Igor is so comfortable with his body, he takes a full part in any activity and never sits on the sidelines watching." Igor's worries had been laid to rest as well. "I'm having a brilliant time with my parents," he said at the time. "It's been great seeing them. It has been even better than I could have imagined. I'm really happy and so are they." At last, his world was complete.

"I didn't sleep the week before we went to England," recalls Elena, reflecting two years later on the momentous events of that remarkable week in 2003. "I had been so worried about the meeting. I was in turmoil about all we had been through with losing Igor and finding him again, but within five minutes of meeting Igor I was no longer worried: I realised that at last everything was now complete in my family. There were no empty spaces in the chain any more. Andre felt the same way as me, and he has become much more relaxed about expressing his feelings since meeting Igor. We both returned to Belarus full of pride for our son; that he had grown up to be quite a clever boy and that he looked more healthy than we had thought possible. We were very glad for Igor, and we felt very secure about his future in the UK. It was clear to us that he would become a good person. We are very happy that he has found himself living that particular life, but of course my heart nearly stopped when we had to say goodbye to each other at the airport. To say goodbye to your own son after such a short visit, after such a long separation ... These were difficult feelings to have. We wanted to be with him longer, to have him come home with us. But at last the stone had dropped from our shoulders completely."

Those who witnessed the reunion saw how enriching it had been, none more so than Victor. "What comes to mind is that when Igor met his parents it was really as if they had known each other all their lives," he says. "I do not believe that you can break a family bond. Igor told his brother, who is nearly six feet tall, that he was older than him and that he must obey him! And Igor told me that he was glad he met his parents, that they are nice people and that he did not know now why he had been so worried about meeting them. Elena is a very intelligent person and was full of tears of awoken emotions. Andre was calm and proud and could not take his eyes away from his son. It was a day never to be forgotten, and I felt proud of my achievement in finally making this happen. Both parents were proud of what Igor himself had achieved in spite of the setbacks he had suffered from radiation. His brother and sister felt acceptance for their elder brother. It was wonderful to see a family together for the first time, reunited after so many years. A wrong committed by the Soviet Union had been put right."

Elena praises the sensitive way that Victor handled the entire process of preparing Andre and her to meet their son. "We met Victor often before we came to the UK which helped us to gradually come to terms with, and to be able to deal with, all that has happened. From the very first contact we developed very warm feelings for Victor, and he became a very dear person in our family. Everything happened because of him and he had to take some hard decisions, but he was always there in the background, doing whatever was needed. He progressed at just the right pace so that this discovery didn't fall on our heads at all once. We understood that everyone needed time to prepare for the meeting, and he enabled us to be in touch with Igor long before we met him. If it was difficult for us to meet Igor, it was even harder psychologically for him to cope with meeting us. But because of Victor's sensitivity, no one has been damaged in mind or health. My parents both died before we found Igor; Victor has become like a father to me."

Elena was also full of gratitude for Barbara's daily care of Igor. "She is a most close and dear person to us because she looked after Igor as he grew up with her. She told us everything about Igor's life in England, step by step. She showed us photographs and explained everything about them, and she took us to the centres where he had had treatment. Barbara was like a real mother for Igor; she gave him everything that mothers give their children. She has done everything correctly and with love for him."

Barbara was also reassured having met Elena and Andre. "I can't imagine life without Igor," she told the television crew after the reunion. "When his real parents were found, I was nervous. What if they wanted him back? But when I met them I realised how happy they were that he was in England. They believe his life is better than it would have been if he'd stayed with them. It shows how much they love him."

Enabling Igor to meet his family and discover that he was neither given away nor abandoned by them, but was instead forcibly removed by a state where human rights were considered inconsequential, has been a wonderful conclusion to Victor's involvement in Igor's life. He hopes that as the time passes, Igor will come to understand the significance of what he was able to do for him. But if he does not, then Victor will always have the satisfaction of knowing that he did right by Igor. "We look after these children to help them. No one has the right to separate or keep a family apart, whether it is an individual or a state organization. I do not think that an adolescent can cope with such enormous decisions when so much appears to be at stake. That's why I had to step in and make some tough decisions on his behalf. I would have liked us all to have worked together using shared common sense, but I understand that sometimes emotions run too high for that to be possible."

The Judge at the Wardship hearing, who had determined that Igor should meet his parents, had also asked Victor to make an application for Igor to become a British citizen, paperwork that Victor had long hoped to secure. Eight years earlier, Victor had applied to the Immigration Department for Igor to be granted Indefinite Leave to Remain in the United Kingdom. Now he set out to obtain British Citizenship on Igor's behalf enabling Igor to stay in the UK for the rest of his life, gaining all the normal rights and responsibilities of a British citizen. Obtaining British nationality is not easy. There is a great deal of documentation to be raised. Victor prepared all the paperwork and on 7 October 2003 he sent off the completed forms and necessary fees to the Immigration Nationality Department.

"Igor was still a minor, therefore his birth parents had to complete part of the forms agreeing to their son changing his nationality," explains Victor. "Without their approval and support, this change in nationality could not happen." Fortunately, both Elena and Andre quickly saw the significance of the opportunity for Igor and had agreed to complete the forms. Says Elena, "I was happy he had the chance to become a British citizen. I understand how much time has now passed since he left Belarus, and I know he will have more opportunities there than in Belarus. He has met many good, kind people and I know he is not alone. Igor is now old enough to make his own decisions in life. I want him to know he is always welcome in Belarus and particularly at our home."

On the 15 December 2003, among Victor's 69th birthday cards, the postman delivered a brown manila envelope. "Inside was the best birthday present I have ever received," remembers Victor. "A letter telling me that Igor's application had been successful and that he was now a British citizen."

The Return

Gaining British citizenship – and a British passport – cleared the way for Igor to make a momentous journey back to the land of his birth. "Once he had seen his parents in the UK, and it went so well with them, it was time to start working for him to go and see his native country and to remove the enormous fear he had of it," explains Victor. "When his parents visited in 2003, we laid the seed that eventually Igor could go and visit them in Belarus." Two years later, and the time had come. In the spring of 2005, shortly after Igor's eighteenth birthday, it was agreed that preparations could be made for Igor to visit his family in Belarus and, on 3 July 2005, Barbara and Igor flew to Belarus together for a week's holiday. The Charity booked and paid for both the airline seats and visas to enable Igor to have the chance to visit the country of his birth, and to spend some time with his parents in the village that should have been his home. Elena had waited eighteen years to take her son home with her, and now it was about to happen. "When we had said goodbye at the airport in London I knew for certain that we would keep in touch, and that we would see each other again," she says. "Anna in particular was always writing to Igor and sending presents via Victor, and letters from Igor were delivered to us from Victor, already translated into Russian. Most teenage boys don't like to write letters, but he wrote to us. Not very often, but enough! He would write about what he was doing and about his plans for the future."

Victor decided that it would be best for Barbara to accompany Igor on this emotional journey. A request to accompany them from Zeneth Entertainment, the TV production company who had been commissioned to make an updated documentary about Igor's life, was turned down in order to keep this first meeting private, although a few months later Igor and Barbara did return for a few days' filming.

"We had been looking forward to Igor's visit for so long," remembers Elena of their first meeting on Belarussian soil. "We flew to the airport on the wings of happiness. While we were waiting for Igor and Barbara we were very worried about how it would all go, but Igor looked very calm and happy to see us, and we immediately took them home. We wanted to make it as much like a holiday as possible. We didn't want to show them too much, but to find the right balance so they could also rest and just be with family." Unfortunately, Elena had just started a new job and was very disappointed that she wasn't allowed to take the week off work, although most days she managed to come home at lunchtime to prepare food and spend an hour with her family. Andre's 20-year-old nephew Sacha was on hand throughout the week to act as translator. Elena explains that there weren't any difficulties communicating despite the language barrier. "When the children didn't understand what they were trying to say, they would gesture with their hands. At other times, Sacha would collect them all together and help explain what everyone wanted from one another. Of course it is a pity that my children cannot speak to each other in one language, but I hope that Anna will continue with her English studies and will soon be able to talk to Igor, and help us talk to him too. She is learning English at school and is very interested in the language, particularly as she now has an English brother."

The week passed quickly and was full of special moments. Andre took his family to see local sights, including war memorials and churches, and they visited a military museum where Igor had a great time exploring a display of tanks. One night the family went to a Belarussian concert, followed by a village disco at which Andre danced with Barbara. "We had fun until 1pm when the mosquitoes sent us to bed," laughs Elena. Later, Igor also met his paternal great-grandmother while in Belarus. "She cried continually, but they were tears of happiness and love," says Elena, explaining that strong family bonds are of great consequence in Belarussian society. "We showed Igor photographs of different relatives, and he was very interested in everything. Every relative we visited cried because they were happy that at last we had our son back."

Igor's parents also made sure that there was plenty of time spent at home just enjoying each other's company. Barbara picked strawberries from the family's vegetable patch while the children set up a basketball ring. Then they all went swimming in one of the many lakes near the village, taking advantage of the very summery warm weather. One night all three Pavlovets children went fishing with their father, taking a small boat to the biggest lake near the village. Igor and Andre spent some time fishing alone together, far from the shore, while the other children swam. "Igor was so proud and happy when he caught two fish," remembers Elena who had prepared a picnic. The family then made a campfire and sat chatting by the flames as dusk fell. "We spent a lovely evening there, talking and just being together. I liked that night very much," she says. Other evenings were spent enjoying Elena's carefully prepared feasts of Belarussian home cooking – paté, meats, potato pancakes and many different salads – before the entire family strolled around the lakes near the village for an hour or two. "It was a holiday for us as well because usually there is a lot of work to do around the house and farm," explains Elena, who continued to get up at 4.30am most mornings to milk the cows and feed the pigs before work.

"Every parent is happy to see their children playing happily together, and here were my three children doing just that. Andre and I were the happiest people at that time watching Igor fully integrate with our two other children. It wasn't like he had just arrived a couple of days before, it was as if he had been there all the time; there was such a naturalness between them and a real aura of happiness that we had not felt before," recalls Elena. "It was a very special and unique energy. Andre's niece was with them as well, and they all stuck together, being comfortable company for Igor. The most important thing for us all was to help him to feel really relaxed, with lots of laughing and joking. To give him the happiest experience possible, to enable him to feel truly free and on holiday."

On the Friday before Igor left, Elena was able to take a day off work and the family went to Minsk together. "I didn't want them to go back to England without any presents," she says with a smile. They then walked around the old town. The following day, the entire extended family, including some relatives who had been working during the week and who had not yet had a chance to meet Elena and Andre's prodigal son, went for an all-day picnic and barbeque in a forest of beech trees. "There were twenty-five of us, including Andre's aunties and cousins, and my sister, nieces and their children," recalls Elena happily. "The children played football, the adults played volleyball, and we all talked to each other. We were a normal family, doing normal things and the day passed so quickly."

That night, as Barbara and Igor were packing their suitcases, they told Elena that they had only good feelings about their visit. "Barbara told me that at last she had found a place where she can have very nice and quiet holidays," laughs Elena. "When she came to Belarus she came as a relative, the door of our house is always open to her. I feel very close to her, and I believe that she feels the same about me. I want Igor to know that he always has a home with us should he want it. The more he visits, the better. Our house is Igor's house."

Today

Igor has accepted his disabilities and is as determined as ever to enjoy his independence. "I always try and work out how to do things but if I can't do it, I'm not afraid to ask for help," he said last year. "People do stare at me still but I don't notice it any more. Kids tend to make comments and their parents will tell them to shut up, but I let it go. It's okay to be different." He decided many years ago not to use the prosthetic devices that he originally came to the UK to be fitted with. Although he stands three feet tall and will not grow any taller, Igor's left arm is as powerful as ever. Last year he amazed the owners of a go-cart track with his deft ability to control the feisty little machines. He passed his driving test first time, in a car with specially extended pedals, and he now drives an adapted Motability car of his own. It has a device on the steering column that enables him to use all the internal controls with his single hand. "I can now go out and come home when I want to," he says. "One day I'll have loads of girls in my car. Three in the back, and one in the front. I'll be sorted."

His bedroom in the Surrey home he shares with Barbara and Roy is that of a typical young man's. There are hip-hop CDs, model cars and posters of glamour models on the walls. "I grew up a lot recently," says Igor. "I went to college, had a girlfriend and met my family for the first time. I want to show everyone that I can make it on my own. I don't know much about Chernobyl – it's sad, but it's all in the past now. I want to look to the future. I have been given some great chances in life. I want to make the most of them."

When Elena came over to help update this book last November, she spent time with Igor in the evenings. "When I look at him, he looks like a fish in water. He can do everything. He drives, he introduced us to his friends, and he has girlfriends as well. He is a fully normal person. I know that as time goes on he will continue to develop."

Victor agrees that Igor's personality has always overwhelmed his handicap. "You don't look at Igor as a disabled boy, you see him as a complete person," he says. And, having met his mother, father, brother and sister, Igor now feels more complete too. Says Victor, "It is wonderful to know that he can now continue with his life, knowing that he was not given away, neglected and unloved, by his parents. The fact that Igor now has roots to his biological family is a reality I could never have dared to imagine when I first met that courageous boy in a Belarussian hospital all those years ago."

Igor still faces challenges in the future. He is hoping for a career in motor racing, after studying mechanics for a year and having a work-experience placement at a motor sports centre. "If they just give me a chance, I'll show them what I can do. I feel really good when I'm driving and I'm capable of a lot more than people think," he has said. Victor has tried encouraging him to learn to use a computer, but Igor remains adamant that cars will provide his future. Igor's surrogate parents and his birth parents are united in their hope that the right opportunity will emerge, and enable Igor to thrive. "Igor has told me that he will try and study hard and I am confident that, in time, he will find a job that satisfies him," explains Elena, who says she now regards her eldest son like any normal parent contemplating her child: "You are there to say 'well done' for what he does and to bless him with good luck in what he has yet to do. I feel as if everything has found its natural place. I have three children. Sometimes they are away from home and sometimes the family is together. I now know that our lives are as they should be."

I ask whether it remains painful to know how many years she was denied with her eldest son. Sighing and taking a moment to consider her reply, she says, "The pain of losing Igor after his birth was almost impossible to bear. When we read about him in the newspaper in 1993, the pain started up again with a new strength. It hurt more then because we knew a bit about him, but not enough to find him. I am not a child. I understand that you can't have everything you want straight away, and as soon as we met Victor we started to calm down, because gradually we started to know something about Igor and his life. From that moment we began to have hope that one day we would see him again."

She tells me that during Igor's visit to Belarus the family were able to celebrate Kupalle, the mid-summer pagan celebration of the country's fertility, together. "This is an historic all-night holiday celebrated each year on 6 July, at which we light bonfires and search for the miraculous flower of the Paparats fern." The plant does not produce flowers, but a legend says that one day it will bloom with wonderful, fiery colour, revealing hidden treasures, and that the person who finds it will be the happiest person in the world. "We no longer need to search for it," says Elena smiling widely. "Our flower came from England."

How You Can Help

If you have been moved by Igor's story and would like to support the continued work of Chernobyl Children Life Line, donations of money and air miles are very gratefully received. The charity was founded in 1991 to help the children of Belarus, that received 70 per cent of the contamination from the world's worst nuclear disaster. Chernobyl Children Life Line has so far enabled 42,000 Belarussian children to come to the UK for respite holidays and set up many projects helping poor families in Belarus. During the past fifteen years more than sixty children have attended school in the UK for one academic year. There are also many children at Belarussian universities supported financially by their dedicated host families in the UK.

Doctors in the republic are experienced, but lack resources. They give CCLL every assistance in helping their children. Since 1992 the charity has shipped many tonnes of medicines, food, toys and clothing to Belarus. With the kind support of Belavia Airlines, each child who visits the UK returns home with thirty kilos of aid.

Donations should be sent to:

Chernobyl Children's Lifeline
6 Hartley Business Park
Selborne Road
Alton
Hampshire
GU34 3HD

Tel.: 01420 511 700

Victor Mizzi, chairman and founder of Chernobyl Children Life Line, is also always pleased to hear from volunteers who would like to be host parents. They should be prepared to invite into their homes two children for one month. Every week that the children stay with host families in Britain, breathing uncontaminated air and eating safe food will improve their damaged immune systems.

Dr Zolovok, director of the children's hospital in Soligorsk, Belarus, says, "Every child taken to the UK for one month is 'returned' two years of life. We are hostages to the hazardous aftermath of radiation. The future of our very race is threatened with extinction as our children, our gene pool, are seriously ill. In the midst of this tragedy we have been given hope by the people of the UK. Thank you for supporting the lives of our children."

Chernobyl Children Life Line now has 145 Links across Britain. Each Link has its own committee whose objective is to raise funds, find and vet host families. The charity welcomes new members, either to raise money for the children's airfares or to welcome them into their homes. Many host families become so attached to the Belarussian children that they pay to bring them over regularly every year. Some also visit their adopted families in Belarus. CCLL wants to continue to expand and create more Links in all areas of the British Isles. Therefore if you think you can offer help in this way, please write and the charity will give you every assistance.

The charity's intention is to bring a minimum of 3000 children a year to the UK, as well as supplying specific individuals in Belarussian hospitals with vital medicine. Igor is not the only child to have been given long-term support and care in Britain by CCLL. The McCaffrey family and the Porter family fostered leukaemia sufferers Marina Ivanovna Grablevskaya and Victoria Sheleg, and Vassilly Kurbuco who has congenital deformities. Victor Bobr has a growth disorder and has been fostered by a family in Jersey. Sergei Kancena and Olga Kohneko are now British subjects following the charity's support. Victor and Birgitta Mizzi have had two boys from the contaminated area, Antom Karatkevichi and Artom Marshalkovinski, living with their family for the past 10 years, both of whom are now at university in Britain.

An estimated 3,800,000 people were living in the area showered with radioactive fall-out following the Chernobyl disaster and at least 600,000 people, including 250,000 children, received high doses of radiation. In November 2004, Swiss Medical Weekly published the findings of the Clinical Institute of Radiation Medicine in Minsk, which showed that the cancer rate had risen in Belarus by 40 per cent between 1990 and 2000. In the Gomel region, the most heavily contaminated area in the country, this figure is 55 per cent. Many of these cancers are of the stomach, rectum or bladder, suggesting that it is the food people eat which is the most significant contributory cause. Children living within 80 miles of the abandoned reactor are 55 times more likely to develop thyroid cancer than the average Russian.

In addition, three million acres of agricultural land in Ukraine, Belarus and the Russian Federation were poisoned. Although more than 100,000 people eventually became environmental refugees from the zone near the nuclear plant, scientists say radiation levels reached more than 12 times the safety levels in areas far outside the danger zone. At the time of the disaster, officials said that only 32 people were killed. They later admitted that the figure had been nearer 300. But experts predict the final death toll to be much higher. The United Nations has described the Chernobyl disaster as an "unprecedented laboratory for human suffering".

The contamination across the south and east of Belarus remains between 14 and 70 times as high as the average for the whole of the country, according to the latest figures in the Journal of Radioactivity. Recent studies have also suggested an increase in "mutations in germ line cells" (congenital deformities) in children whose parents were exposed to radiation in Belarus, according to Keith Baverstock, a radiation scientist from the University of Kuopio in Finland, who used to be a radiation advisor to the World Health Organisation and who was instrumental in uncovering the impact of Chernobyl on human health.

British neurosurgeon Jenny Haley is highly experienced but was shocked by what she saw on her trip to Belarus in the mid 1990s. "I've never seen children born without an eye or with such grossly deformed hips in my life," she said. "I've seen children with small heads in the course of my work, but these are much more severe cases."

Dr Nica Gress, a senior health adviser to the Belarus government, is calling for mass scanning of foetuses and twice yearly checks on schoolchildren. "Even children who live 300 miles away from the reactor are developing chronic illnesses," she says.

For Belarussian children coming to the UK on a respite holiday, the experience is as exciting as a British youngster visiting Disneyland. Most of the things we take for granted, even simple things like ice cream and DVDs, can be new and tantalizing experiences to these grateful children. Their parents write ecstatically to the British host families when their children return home.

Thank you very much for your attention to our son. During the month in England he changed not only outwardly, but inwardly as well. He has become more independent and grown up. My child was operated on for a brain tumour five years ago. But the tumour was not removed. I am terrified by what awaits him in the future, there are no drugs for his form of tumour. The only rescue is clean air and food. But we have neither. I am convinced that the month spent in England is very beneficial to him. This month left me with hope that there are many kind people on our planet who care about my son, just as I do.

From the Borshachevski family

Thanks a lot for taking care of our children. Our son Anton returned home in good health. He got stronger and weighs four kilogrammes more now. Frankly speaking we worried greatly when Anton was not at home for a month and so far away. But when we met him at the airport we understood that everything was fine. Anton was very happy in his English family. Every day he tells us something interesting about his trip. How wonderful it is that there are such people in your country who help the children of Belarus.

From the Somokish family

English people with their love and care help to return health to our children, and give us mothers both moral and material support. It's very important to know that there are persons who try to make our pain easier. We can almost believe all the problems will be disappeared and our son will be healed and we'll be happy together. Kostya came back in better condition and good spirit. His blood analysis shows better results now. I could never manage our problems alone. Here Kostya often feels bad and catches cold. After visiting England he gets new forces to resist diseases. It's impossible to express gratitude to people who help our children to survive. There are not a lot of people who may and want to share other's pain. In January, in Kostya's brain new swelling was found. We hope this is not a cancer swelling. We don't know yet. I hope this will be clarified after examination. Then we'll be able to make some plans for the future. Thank you, nice people.

From the Orlov family

For the sympathetic British families who devote their time and energy to helping these children, such grateful and emotive letters make it all worthwhile.

In 1996, Victor Mizzi was awarded Belarus's highest order, Frantsysk Skaryna, named after the Belarussian inventor of the printing press. It has also been awarded to Linda Walker, of Chernobyl Children's Project UK.

Chernobyl Children Life Line
Charity Reg: 1014274
Inland Revenue: XN88971

www.chernobylchildlifeline.org

Bibliography

Chernobyl and Nuclear Power in the USSR, David Marples (Macmillan)

Truth About Chernobyl, Grigorii Medvedev (Tauris)

Children of Chernobyl: Human Cost of the World's Worst Nuclear Disaster, Adi Roche (Fount)

The Republic of Belarus: Nine Years After Chernobyl, Situation, Problems, Actions, Semeshko and Antsypov (Ministry for Emergencies and Population Protection from the Chernobyl Catastrophe)

Children and Women of Belarus: Today and Tomorrow (CEE/CIS Baltic States Section, Unicef)

Chernobyl: The Forbidden Truth, Taroshinskaya and Sallabank (Carpenter)